Maureen Duffy was b
College, London. She is
her works of fiction inc
Eye, The Microcosm, The
Want to Go to Moscou
Londoners. Her volumes o. poetry are Lyrics for the Dog Hour,
The Venus Touch, Evesong and Memorials for the Quick and the
Dead. She has also written three non-fiction books: The Erotic
World of Faery, The Passionate Shepherdess: Aphra Behn 1640-89
and Inherit the Earth: A Social History. Maureen Duffy was a
co-founder of the Writers' Action Group, and is Chairman
of the Authors Lending and Copyright Society, and Vice-
Chairman of the British Copyright Council. She lives in
London.

MAUREEN DUFFY

Men and Beasts

An Animal Rights Handbook

Granada Publishing

Paladin Books
Granada Publishing Ltd
8 Grafton Street, London W1X 3LA

First published by Paladin Books 1984

ISBN 0-586-08464-9

Reproduced, printed and bound in Great Britain by
Hazell Watson & Viney Limited,
Aylesbury, Bucks

Set in Baskerville

For Nello

With the exception of 'Chattel' and 'Bullocks' all the poems in this volume have been published in *Memorials of the Quick and the Dead* by Maureen Duffy.

Contents

Preface and Acknowledgements

Why yet another 'animal book', the potential reader may ask. Surely the existing texts, especially Ryder's *Victims of Science* and Singer's *Animal Liberation* both of which were reissued in 1983 and are the two classics of what has come to be almost a literary sub-genre, cover the ground more than adequately. My excuse is that I have tried not to re-hash other people's arguments or material but to put forward my own views in the hope that this may attract new converts to the animal rights cause and yet provide a handy pocket book that the converted can carry about with them.

The process of changing the climate of thought in any area of human activity is a long one and usually a matter of slow attrition rather than overnight conversion. Many books need to be written, a topic must be constantly brought to the public attention in every possible way before progress can be made. In this book I have put forward a deliberately rationalist, practical viewpoint that is nevertheless avowedly partisan and, I hope, makes clear that I regard being a vegetarian and conducting my life in common cause with the other animals, if necessary against members of my own species, as a perfectly rational, uncranky way to live.

I became a vegetarian out of respect for someone else's views; I have remained one out of respect for my own. I began by phasing out first meat and then fish over a period of several months. If I felt like eating flesh I did so until I no longer experienced those appetites as stronger than my desire not to collude with the death of the creature I was eating and the industry that had brought it about. I have now been a vegetarian for seventeen years. I don't know if it has benefitted my health. I certainly feel no worse for it and I suspect, although I can't of course prove it, that I might by now have felt much worse if I had gone on eating meat in quantity.

Occasionally I still get a craving for some remembered delicacy, usually fish or shellfish with its strong childhood Friday tea associations. Smells of cooking meat or fish can still make me salivate but the remembered sensations of the textures of flesh in the mouth are a fairly strong antidote. However, I reserve my right should I ever be stranded on that hypothetical desert island to exercise my biological instinct for survival as a unique unit by killing for nourishment like any other carnivore if there is no other way to survive. I don't say I should be able to exercise that right on my own behalf, although I probably could for another, but I nevertheless reserve it as a rational choice.

I am not, as some of my vegetarian friends are, physically squeamish about carcases or bits of them, only about their premature and probably painful manner of dying. I was brought up to gut fish, fowl and rabbit and to take pride in the craft of doing it. That ability has stayed with me. Even so I shy away from butchers' shops because behind the hung corpse I can always see the living creature with its interest, charm or beauty, and when I encounter a farm animal in the fields I see not only the breathing, warm beast with its moist eye and lively movements but the carcase it must soon become. The only thing that makes such knowledge bearable is the thought that they don't share it and that, at least as far as I can manage in an omnivorous society, I am not party to their deaths.

Becoming a vegetarian often alters, at least for a time, the human's way of seeing other animals. While I was still eating them, it was as if a veil hung between us, as if I saw them through glass or transparent plastic. There was no real warmth or intimacy in my perception of members of other species unless they were household pets, and even then there was a numbing knock-on effect from my non-perception of meat animals to their domestic relatives, a distancing which is at its strongest in the vivisector.

I didn't move from a fondness for animals to not eating

them but in the opposite direction, from the conscious reasoned decision to become a vegetarian to a greater perception of individual creatures and a heightened response to them, and this although I already shared my life with a dog. When I gave up eating them I experienced for a time a state of almost hyperaesthesia whenever I looked at a non-human. They seemed to glow, to radiate warmth and life once I had lost the desensitizing film that had been necessary to cover my eyes while I went on eating meat. This has become in its turn a consciousness of their individual existence, of each one not as member of a herd or species but as a unique biological unit like me, with its own will to life and happiness that in humans we dignify as rights.

This book is my contribution towards the growing movement for a general recognition of that uniqueness. I have tried to keep it easily assimilable without the use of footnotes. At the end the reader will find a list of recommended books for further reading, divided roughly according to the main sections of the book, which supplement my own views or approach the same question from a different angle. Throughout I have also raised questions and made suggestions for the progress of animal liberation. I don't expect these to be necessarily agreed with but I hope they will provoke discussion both inside and outside the movement.

Because these are very much my own views I take full responsibility for them but I must acknowledge the help I have had both from organizations and individuals. In particular I should like to thank Pauline McKenna and Animal Aid for their most valuable assistance, Compassion in World Farming, The National Anti-Vivisection Society, Angela Walder and the British Union for the Abolition of Vivisection, the RSPCA, M. Seymour-Rouse of Euro-group, Ronnie Lee and the Animal Liberation Front for permission to reprint the material in Appendix A, Richard Ryder for reading the chapter on vivisection and T. B. Vesey for making many helpful suggestions in the chapter on farming.

ACCIDENT

Ahead a bird gunned down by the car in front
that spirts away in a burst of pain and feathers
flutters to the roadside. Anytime it might be me
bucking the breath out of a soft body
with my metal hide
I sic myself on to retrieve
knowing I should cure or kill.
Undistinguished, pied like cheap bathroom lino
one in a million it drags its maimed leg
from my reach behind the wire gate
sets a bead on me with painted still life
bright eye I can't put out
shuffles with beggarly speed into a crater
for cover from my murdering touch.

'Beware guard dogs. Keep out.'
The notice barks overhead.
I remind myself of the common fall of sparrows.
'If we're that way,' the phone voice says kindly,
'after a dog that's been knocked down . . .'

There is a hierarchy in suffering.
The child next door dies wept by a street
while hundreds let fall their dried bundles of limbs
unremarked; my pigeon drags its broken claw
across my chest as a thousand broilers
slit their throats for the Sunday roast.

Yet I can't nod it off. It was afraid
of me and fear I understand.
When I go back it's dead
the head fallen awry, the feathers
softened to down. The dogs will find it.
It has attained, of course, a peace
in its hunched nothingness
and someone has thoughtfully painted over
the sharp eye with a fold of lead.

I know in the block beyond
the surgeon is fitting his scalpel
into the flesh of a man, a child run down this morning
drains vicarious life from a slung bottle

that the splinter of pain that stabbed
these ounces of hollow bone and feather
in this corner of the grounds
where they are building the new ward
is not a breath in the tempest of terror.

But it was afraid and I couldn't explain.
It was dying my death while for a moment
I died a bird. No sophistry of profit
or the fitness to survive
no humanity can absolve me from that communion
of animal fear
nor one pain cancel out another
though it go to the morning dustcart
expendable as cheap torn lino.

1 Introduction

I grew up in a meat-eating world, that is one in which those who could afford to eat flesh did so and those who couldn't aspired to. It was a world in which the only junk food was fish and chips, and pie or eels and mash. English traditional cooking was still the norm. Spaghetti was eaten only by immigrants; pizza was unknown. Our vegetables were boiled tasteless and nutritionless and it was the meat which gave our food any savour. In consequence, when I was a child I ate almost nothing except as much meat as I could scrounge. On meatless days I preferred to go without or hope for better things from tea; a bloater, winkles or fried roe either in globular slabs or the soft pâté on toast.

In this world the omelet belonged to a different class which, it was thought, could afford such elegant restraint because of the amount of roast game it consumed for the rest of the time. Meat was 'goodness'. A meal that didn't contain it hadn't 'a bit of *goodness* in it'.

Meat was not only the chief source of flavour in our diet, it was felt to be almost magically the chief source of virtue. We knew very little of vitamins and proteins. There was food to fill you up which was largely white bread covered by some layer of sweetening: syrup, white sugar, jam or chocolate spread. It was understood that the purpose of this was to stuff the stomach against hunger. For growth and health the intake of flesh was necessary as if by eating a dead animal its strength and powers were transferred to you.

Tradition, history and what was known of the behaviour of the rich reinforced this. There was the roast beef of Old England that had made her great, especially in Elizabethan times and the gargantuan dinners of Mrs Beeton consumed by Victorian empire builders. The upper classes, we believed, ate roast swan, venison, trout and turbot. Logically, if they could afford the best and that was what they ate, those foods must be the acme of desirability and nutrition.

In order to be eaten meat must, by and large, be killed. Again we saw or knew by hearsay of the mass annual slaughter of fish and fowl by 'huntin' and shootin''. In our turn, and on a lesser scale we also took part in killing. Chickens had their necks wrung by granny, rabbits were hung up and karate chopped, shellfish went live into boiling water, eels were held down writhing and cut up in pieces.

This all seemed part of necessity, of our way of life that had to maximize every available source of food if we were ourselves to survive. However, because we are imaginative and rationalizing animals, as I grew up I had to try to find a sufficient justification for this carnivorous course.

I was partly urged towards this by the opening up of the English palate to what I had been brought up to regard as 'messed up foreign food'. I found on my first visit to France in my teens that I actually preferred it. Italy reinforced this. Furthermore, with the springing up of Italian coffee bars all over London an alternative to meat and two veg became easily available. The eating habits of the whole nation were in process of change. Cornflakes replaced bacon for breakfast, and the introduction of the fridge and prepacked food, together with a general rise in living standards, had as much effect on our culinary customs as jeans and the washing machine did on our dress.

I still saw, however, no reason to become a vegetarian. The sufferings and deaths of the animals I ate quite simply didn't imaginatively exist for me. Nevertheless, I needed some explanation of the world which included meat eating. There were several open to me and I think I adopted them all in turn.

The most obvious was the orthodox religious standpoint, represented in this country mainly by Judaeo-Christianity and including the beliefs of Islam about mankind's relationship to the other animals. This attitude has been extensively analyzed by others and I don't intend to repeat that exercise at length here. Briefly, the Bible, principally the Book of Genesis in the Old Testament, gives man, on God's authority, dominion over the other animals and the right to use them for his benefit.

The New Testament, particularly in the story, whether seen as parable or miracle, of the use of a herd of pigs to receive the devils cast out of a human by Jesus which then kill themselves in a lemming-like rush over a cliff, does nothing to counter the Old Testament view.

Non-human animals did derive one benefit from Christianity in that the emphasis on a contrite spirit as the sacrifice desired by God did free them from the altar stone and sacrificial knife of classical religion. However, both Judaism and Islam continued to prescribe bloody methods of ritual slaughter to ensure that meat was acceptable for consumption in the eyes of God and man.

Compassion for fellow creatures is often claimed for St Francis but Peter Singer has pointed out that Francis's concern extended to the whole world, animate and inanimate alike, and doesn't therefore form a rational basis for an ethic of equality for all sentient creatures. Humans, though, don't behave in a strictly logical way, and Francis's generalized charity has often lessened the sufferings of individual animals, especially when it has been taken as an antidote to the extreme, Christian belief that because only man has a soul the fate of other beings is unimportant.

The Judaic insistence on a single god, consisting of a human appearance as father and patriarch, and a spirit, which corresponds to man's apprehension of himself as a psyche imprisoned in a house of bone and flesh, was probably emphasized partly to preserve the sense of nationhood, of separateness from surrounding peoples, many of whom had either pantheons of deities, eponymous gods of city states, or a combination of the two, often with non-human attributes or manifestations. In particular the Egyptians, among whom of course the Jews spent a long formative period of exile, represented several of their deities as hybrids, part human and part dog, cat, bull or bird.

The monotheistic anthropomorphic tradition which has

come to dominate the Western world, replacing the original native pantheons of Celts and Teutons as well as Romans and Greeks, has encouraged a rigid separation between man and his cousins. In countries where this hasn't been so, as for example the Hindu parts of the East, including its offshoots of Buddhism and Jainism, vegetarianism and a respect for all life has often been linked to religious belief.

What I will call the separatist tradition has always been particularly strong in Roman Catholic countries with their emphasis on the unique importance of the human soul and their social and economic problems of over-population and poverty. If it weren't for the Hindu experience, it might be argued that vegetarianism and a concern for other animals is an indulgence of the affluent.

It was St Thomas Aquinas who gave the stronger authority to the doctrine than non-human animals do not possess an immortal soul. This idea surfaced again in Descartes' mechanistic view that they also had no mind, no seat of sentiency and therefore were mere automata. Pavlovian behaviourism continues this idea into modern times.

The truth is surely that this line of convenience thinking is simply a rationalization from the *status quo*, and a justification for continuing it, much like any other argument in favour of an established system of inequality. It can't be denied that we exercise dominion over the other beasts, and arguments can of course always be found to support it, as they were found for slavery, and against universal education and suffrage. If man is made in God's image then *ipso facto* God is made in man's and will hand down tenets to suit his maker.

Significantly, it was to a herding and farming people that this sway was given. Hunter gatherers, until they are, in this sense, corrupted by modern civilization, usually seem to show a rather different relationship to the other animals with whom they share their way of life. The hunting anthropoid probably felt the same sort of kinship and near reverence for the creatures he hunted as the Esquimaux. He was after all hunted in his turn and it was easier for him to see himself as part of the natural network of plants and animals covering the earth.

This idea of a whole earth has had its modern counterparts in, for example, Teilhard de Chardin's concept of the biosphere, an elaboration of the Christian concept of a whole creation, and in the image of the nitrogen cycle, best expressed in the poetry of Dylan Thomas.

These theories recognize the interdependence of all animal and plant species in a universal, sometimes almost mystical, complete ecosystem. While they are an advance on 'the lower animals are there for man's use' view in that they express a respect for the rest of nature, they do nothing to advance the cause of animal liberation. Indeed, insofar as they can be invoked to justify the constant tinkering with the present state of nature to restore or maintain a balance which is felt to be good in itself, they support the idea of *management*, which usually means that someone somewhere is about to be 'culled', the current euphemism for killed. The poisoning of thousands of seagulls in the Scottish firths to encourage terns back to their old nesting sites is an example of this, as indeed are most forms of hunting for sport where the avowed motive is number control.

It must have been the introduction of farming which led to the abandonment of respect for other animals and of a perception of humans as one species among many. The other animals became truly subservient when they lost their freedom both to mate and roam at will. The breeding of herd animals, sheep and goats, and their management must have greatly encouraged the idea of dominion and the theology to support it. Now humans pitted their cunning against other predators not so much in their own defence as in defence of the living chattels that they owned.

The building of towns and cities further emphasized human difference although there were always the hive insects to remind us that architectural organization isn't everything. Taken from their natural habitat to selected pastures and bred for yield and compliance, food animals came to be seen as further and further removed from their masters. This pattern of farming and the responses it engendered is probably in some parts of the world at least ten thousand years engrained in the human consciousness. It's hardly surprising then that it should take so long to change.

Yet such a pattern, however well entrenched in the economic and social structures, isn't immovable nor is it a true basis for an ethical position unless our ethics are to be simply a reflection of what is.

Many people of course do accept this. Their morality is a recognition of prevailing conditions, with minor adjustments made when necessity or common sense dictate. If the norm is to eat meat and benefit by vivisection they will do so out of a general inertia. What is is right and can't be radically changed. Yet moral and ethical revolutions do occur and life itself seems to be a constant struggle between the forces of conservation and change. Slavery, in the sense in which Wilberforce and Fox used the term, has been largely abolished and the Pankhursts would acknowledge that all women in Britain do have the right to vote although in both these cases the achievement of the desired change has made only too clear how much more needs to be done. To change the way of life of millions of our non-human cousins requires an enormous expenditure of energy and, indeed, time. First, the accepted inertia on this question, bred into us by thousands of years of regarding ourselves as not only the dominant species but as having the godlike power of life and death which we have often attributed to our own deities, must be overcome.

Perhaps such a revolution has had to wait for the technological advances that would make it possible. Our hunter-gatherer ancestors lived in a kind of harmonic tension with the rest of nature. They were outnumbered and outclassed in the daily struggle for survival by dozens of other species. Unlike many others they survived the Ice Age in the north while in the warmer parts they had already begun to organize an urban life and develop the new conceptual tool of literacy, to move from hunter to farmer.

The necessary organization of labour and of food production already contains within it the embryo of that factory farming that is our source of cheap food now. Although the life of a goat in a Babylonian herd in neolithic times was undoubtedly pleasanter and freer than that of a battery hen today, the concepts and basic assumptions that governed it were no different from those that order the lives of battery hens. The goat was quite simply a food unit as they are.

It is still not possible to say how the transition from an essentially nomadic hunter-gatherer economy to a sedentary farming one came about, but like it or not, and our current attitudes are a mixture of love and hate, urbanization is at the root of our development. Evolution in man now proceeds not by physical change but by conceptual and technological modifications which have grown directly from that great shift to farming, the mass management of the food supply.

I have used the word 'sedentary' quite deliberately for it was the new habits of life that contributed to the rate of change and brought about Jericho and Mohenjo-daro, Babylon and Tyre. Farming is seasonal. There are fallow periods for both animal and plant. The life of the hunter gatherer is one of almost constant motion. Food must be searched for most days and this activity itself provides interest, movement, communion with others and the world, small rituals to be performed and celebrations of great finds or hunting campaigns.

The husbanding of crop plants and animals is less absorbing of time and interest. (Perhaps this is why modern farmers are keen to preserve an ersatz form of hunting to allay their boredom.) It frees the mind to play and create, to develop arts and sciences which can be preserved by a sedentary urban society. These developments in turn push us in our own minds further from our fellow creatures. The other animals don't write, keep accounts, build libraries or decorate tombs.

Their achievements in these fields are clearly inferior and we have regarded this as giving us the right to use these non-achievers to suit ourselves. In the past, too, we have used this argument to justify the use of what seemed non-achieving humans, blacks and manual workers whether male or female, in various forms of slavery or inequality both of cultural opportunities and of the franchise. That we can, by and large, no longer do so makes it harder to apply to non-humans as well. Once the theory of hierarchy is broken only speciesism is left to justify inhumane treatment for non-humans. It is the last psychological and theoretical barrier that animal liberationists must break.

It has been suggested in recent writings that the instinct for survival may lie not merely in the biological unit itself but is even deeper programmed into the genes. Whatever its source, this very fundamental drive, when coupled with human conceptual powers, becomes speciesism, as Richard Ryder has dubbed it.

As so often, we have taken an animal instinct and elaborated it with a theoretical superstructure. The other animals recognize, at least instinctively, the bounds of their own species. Within it they don't kill each other to eat though they may, as it were at a remove, for breeding or territory, and they usually mate within their own kind. Many of them live together in species communities which are reflections in little of our own. Like us they prey outside the species.

Speciesism, then, is deeply engrained in the animal fabric. There is nothing particularly human about it only, as so often, about our ability to put it into practice. We are quite simply more efficient speciesists than other animals. Our reaction to this can take one of two forms, or indeed may swing between them. We can either shrug and say that because we are animals too we can't be blamed for behaving like the rest, or we can say that with our greater human power of imagination we should be able to choose paths other than merely more efficient forms of speciesism.

This choice is central to the whole question of animal liberation. It springs from the post-Darwinian recognition of both kinship and difference. In accepting that men are animals too we may reinforce the view that no other behaviour can be expected of us than a more efficient version of that common to most sentient creatures: the combination of survival and propagation.

The alternative is to recognize that the quality which makes us different, our heightened power of imagination with all that it brings, is a truly human one (perhaps the only truly human one) and that, in fulfilling it, we are most ourselves. The imaginative faculty which can visualize and conceptualize seems to be an over-development of a survival mechanism like the one which makes squirrels hoard for winter or chimpanzees conceal bananas from each other for later consumption. It is based on the ability to foresee and to picture, but is set free in humans from the trigger programming of season and temperature that puts a hibernator to work.

This faculty, however derived, plays over all our others and over those drives which we share with other species. Animal mothers protect their young. That is one of the most fundamental urges. In humans this instinct becomes the elaboration of maternal and parental love. It dictates that a parent will constantly seek the best for its offspring, including better education and health care than may be available to other people's children. Yet at the same time the imaginative faculty can work to question the application of this drive, can opt for National Health treatment and the local comprehensive for altruistic reasons because the imaginative faculty has been engaged on behalf of the children of others.

Imagination, the truly human faculty, has to be engaged now on behalf of species other than our own. We have to exercise it to put ourselves in our cousins' place in order to modify our attitudes and behaviour towards them. We have almost succeeded in impersonating other oppressed groups within our own species, now it is time to move outside.

This ability of humans which I have chosen to call by a traditional term, and one from my own discipline of writing, imagination, is the same that enables the scientist to hypothesize or the mathematician to embody in symbols. It makes humans construct political systems. It enables us to inhabit the bodies and lives of others, a transference that has to take place for us to begin to understand the need for rights for other animals.

To do so isn't to be sentimental or, that other canard often applied to the so-called 'animal lover', anthropomorphic. Empathy, as Peter Singer has pointed out, needn't even include a great liking for animals but it does mean an ability to impersonate their needs and sufferings and to admit that they have them. The vivisector in his everyday work has to inhibit this faculty in order to continue treating sentient creatures as objects for experiment. This inhibition lies behind that hardening of the heart that even Shakespeare's contemporaries (from *Cymbeline*) noted as the result of trying it on the dog.

> QUEEN: I will try the forces
> Of these thy compounds on such creatures as
> We count not worth the hanging – but none human – ...
> CORNELIUS: Your Highness
> Shall from this practice but make hard your heart.

The rational basis for our empathy with other animals is the recognition of kinship in the theory of evolution. Yet even this is a double-edged weapon that can be turned in our hands, for evolutionary theory includes the often popularly misunderstood concept of the survival of the fittest. In our human egocentricity we have taken this as evolution's stamp of approval on ourselves and our place as we see it at the apex of the evolutionary process, repeating the old God-given dominion in scientific terms.

In reality a seeding of neutron bombs or virulent bacteria across the inhabited parts of the globe could end our fitness to survive tomorrow and leave rats at the top of the evolutionary tree. Survival is no indication of intelligence, merely an ability to have met the physical accidents of life and exploited the environment as land gulls and feral pigeons do.

This kinship with the whole of animal kind brings us ambiguous emotions. We have for so long built into our symbols and our language the idea of 'the beasts' that an acknowledgement of our closeness cannot but be disturbing.

The terms 'animal', 'brute' and 'beast' are all pejoratives. When humans behave badly we say they are behaving like animals even when the comparison is ludicrous. The word has come to mean simply dirty, disgusting, obscene or violent, when used in this way, yet very few animals are any of these things and then only in special circumstances, usually when they have fallen into the hands of men. Most animals are actually rather clean and unaggressive except in pursuit of food or sex, the two imperatives we all share. Man, in common with the orang-utan, has a propensity to rape quite unknown to the gorilla. Some animals, including us, do behave badly.

Our ambiguity is at its strongest in bestiality and vivisection, both of which depend for their existence on this perception of co-existent similarity and difference. It is the fact that man and sheep are different that gives the fetishist his excitement and yet they must be sufficiently alike for the act of bestiality to take place.

Vivisection, bestiality with a scalpel, depends on all biological units being sufficiently alike for the results from other animals to be applied to man, yet for there to be such a species barrier, the difference between humans and the rest, that the infliction of pain and death becomes permissible. The same double-edged perception lay behind the use of the insane, Jews, gypsies, homosexuals and so on for experiments in Nazi concentration camps.

The very concept of sub-species, sub in respect of rights because sub-human, is dangerous both to man and to other animals. It reinforces the idea of hierarchy, that there is a descending scale of humanness and therefore, tied directly to it, of rights. At the bottom are those creatures we find it hardest to empathize with: fish and reptiles. From them the ladder ascends with animals and humans neatly arranged on the rungs until it reaches what any particular society may see as the top: the American WASP or the mythical teutonic pure Aryan, tall, blond-haired and blue-eyed. The small dark, slant-eyed people will find themselves, like the peasants massacred at My Lai, on a low rung barely above the great apes. Significantly this attitude is often accompanied by dehumanizing language. People become 'gooks' or 'yids' as animals become brutes.

What is clear about this ladder is that the further down you find yourself placed, the fewer are your rights, until you stand at the point where they disappear completely. Jews were herded like cattle and trained away. They died as in an abattoir. The concept which allows us to treat other animals as having no rights washes over those humans who come closest to them in the eyes of those who exercise political dominion. Rights are traditionally and supposedly abolished at the species barrier rung but the cut-off can be inched up above this point. What is dangerous to us all is the belief that below a certain level there are no rights.

The concept of hierarchy encourages this. We have to think laterally, to extend the idea of equality sideways to take in other creatures, other species. If we no longer believe that our dominion is God-given, if we acknowledge our historical and biological kinship with other animals, the only concepts that can deny rights to us all are the arguments from necessity, convenience or the *status quo*, none of which is the basis for an ethic.

An ethic demands that we accept certain principles for themselves, however inconvenient, and that the arguments of *status quo* or so-called necessity are seen for what they are: mere convenience. To accord rights to other beings, human or not, requires a certain degree of inconvenience and a rethinking of attitudes.

The first right is that to life. For humans we can leave this right in abeyance, with moral sanction, in conditions of war or self-defence. Yet the right is acknowledged to exist and it takes such special conditions to put it even temporarily into cold storage. With the animals the position is reversed as it was for the humans in concentration camps. The right to life isn't admitted. We regard the lives of other animals as at our, not their disposal.

The right to life underlies all others. It is the basis of the fundamental social contract that allows animals and men to live in groups. I won't kill you and I will trust you not to kill me. The contract breaks down sometimes, even often, in violent crime, private or public, but it remains the thread on which society is strung together. That is, for humans. For other animals we try to palliate our taking away of this right by almost admitting a right not to suffer. As we pick up our pre-packed steaks or chicken pieces we comfort ourselves, if we relate the bits of sanitized flesh to a living, feeling body at all, by the thought that the animals' lives, however short, were comfortable, not too bad really, and ended without pain or suffering.

Neither of these precepts is true, or necessarily so, but we believe them because we must. Most people made to visit a slaughterhouse would, as the late Lord Dowding did, become vegetarian. We go on distancing ourselves by hiding behind the industrial process of farming that we have lived with for thousands of years and that now helps us to make palatable something which is, baldly put, mass murder.

In denying for our own convenience the right to life we have constantly to deny any ethical basis for what we do. Without the right to life all our other rights are null and can't be exercised. We comfort ourselves that other animals don't share man's ability to 'look before and after', especially after. They don't by this line of thinking foresee death. They are happy in their field and not subject to our appalling apprehension.

It's true that the sight of animals contentedly browsing is comforting but does the fact that they don't apprehend death mean that we have the right to cut life off at any moment we determine? Do members of a suddenly discovered aboriginal tribe in a rain forest who don't understand the uniformed figures with flame guns, have no loss, no rights just because they don't understand that fire is about to consume them?

Non-human animals in our power live in this kind of ignorance and die in it, much as the humans in ghettos and even in the camps themselves could hardly accept that those who were led away went not to hospital or another camp but to death. Yet we wouldn't for a moment suggest that, when applied to humans, we have the right to kill those who aren't expecting us to. (Many animals of course live in appalling conditions and die in pain and terror but I will deal with that in a later chapter.)

By what right then do we kill any living creature? We do so because might is right, because we can and it suits us to do so. None of these arguments is acceptable as a justification for killing humans. For our own species we exercise a purely animal discrimination. This, as others have remarked elsewhere, is simple speciesism.

It is sometimes argued in reply that humans have more potential than other creatures. Many writers have pointed out that this doesn't apply to several categories of humans: the senile, the human vegetable, the paralysed. Indeed so little do we regard this argument that we actually try to prevent those who have decided that their lives have no potential from ending them, and we prosecute those who would try to help them to kill themselves in as dignified and painless a way as possible. The widely reported case of James Haig, paralysed from the neck down, who was driven to set fire to the custom-built bungalow he had been moved into, contrasts strongly with the civilized exit of Arthur Koestler.

In this particular respect the gas chambers and experimental laboratories of Nazi Germany have done us an additional, more subtle, harm. The rationale which gave society the right to dispose of the socially and genetically undesirable has made us terrified of admitting again any such reasoning which can be so hideously abused. It causes us to argue that no human may ever be killed and that the human right to life is sacrosanct, though many people are prepared to temper this in the case of early abortion.

The argument for human potential would of course mean, if taken to its logical conclusion, that all abortion was wrong, once sperm and ovum had fused, except where it could be conclusively proved that the resulting being was incapable of sustaining a rewarding human life. Here again we should be in the realms of an argument that most people believe must be modified by common sense and must take account in particular of the right of a woman to make choices about her own life. Humans have seemingly lost, in any reliable way (even if they ever had it), the useful abortive mechanisms that some species retain for removing non-viable foetuses, which may range from those physically deformed to those simply too much for the food supply, by reabsorption into the mother's body or early expulsion from it, or by a period of waiting as a blastocyst until conditions for the survival of the young improve.

As with everything else, humans have had to project from an animal reaction into the levels of imagination and choice to deal with the problems of unwanted (for whatever reason) foetuses. (An argument could perhaps be made from our use of abortion to justify other killings, especially of creatures that we find it convenient to think of as less in intelligence and capacity than a newborn human. No such dangerous spin-off arises with contraception.)

The truth is that our *right* to life as a near absolute, as distinct from its function as part of the social contract, is a projection from the biological unit's instinct for survival which we share with the dolphin, the sparrow and even the hermit crab. There is no logical basis for granting it to a human and not to anyone else with the same innate survival drive unless the human is endowed with a soul that the non-human doesn't have.

On this acknowledged right to life depend the other two which humans have expressed as a political ideal for themselves: liberty and the pursuit of happiness. Once again these are fundamental and universal animal instincts dignified as rights for humans. All creatures struggle to be free. Even domestic pets maintain a constantly shifting balance between freedom and dependence by exercising the choice to remain with us, to come back after a night's hunting or chasing a thrown stick.

The pursuit of personal happiness is also an obvious biological imperative, though what makes an individual animal happy will vary with its needs and conditions. Sometimes it will be sex or food, warmth and comfort, freedom from fear and harassment, the exercise of freedom of movement to run or to lie in the sun. Humans can add to this the exercise of imagination in creation and work. The basic animal pursuit of happiness reads rather like a holiday brochure and it may indeed be part of the reason that such holidays, at their best, give us a positive feeling of sheer well-being. For a time we are almost able to slough off the additional stresses which our humanity imposes on us along with our enhanced capacities.

It is our population explosion that has largely denied their basic needs, our rights, to other animals. Our sheer numbers circumscribe their freedom and deny them its exercise in pursuit of happiness. At the same time we imprison them and mete out such quality of life as we think fit. Perhaps we are envious of that holiday brochure happiness they might enjoy without our interference. Our imaginative capacity is double-edged, it not only enhances it also brings anxiety and boredom such as only caged animals know, and we find it often difficult to enjoy for long what we think of as a life of simple 'animal' hedonism.

In denying the other animals those biological imperatives that we have designated the equal rights of all humans, we automatically condemn the creatures within our control to diminished lives. Curiously, it's those who are biologically closest to us, the mammals, who are most affected. Birds, fish, reptiles and insects for the most part until we decide to kill them, are at least able to exercise liberty and a pursuit of happiness, except of course for those caught up in the food chain like battery hens. The mammals, with whose sufferings we ought to be able to identify most easily because their biological structure is so similar to our own, are those whom we mistreat the most for our own convenience. It almost seems as if there might be a clue to this behaviour in the fact that when chimpanzees hunt, their prey is very often a monkey, though as far as I know only man has regularly practised cannibalism. Perhaps the very similarity of mammal to man makes it necessary for us to emphasize the difference, to play down our cousinhood.

The rights which we accord our fellow humans we give each other in recognition of that social contract I mentioned earlier which enables us to live together in urban complexity. To extend them to other animals would require a desire from us to live in a similar harmony with them. The basis for this would have to be our recognition of a need for this on our part that isn't, as at present, a need merely to exploit them. We should have to envisage a world that had a true ecological balance. Christians might find the Franciscan attitude a basis for such a theoretical position. Of necessity this would mean a more planned world. The by-products of uncontrolled industrial use, effluent, waste, lead in petrol, oil slicks, would no longer be tolerable. Man's freedom to exploit and develop on an *ad hoc* basis would have to be further curtailed. Dominion over would have to be reinterpreted as responsibility for.

The process has already begun, indeed it's as old as urbanization itself, and the rules for burying the dead outside the town or city. Yet many of us are still unwilling to give up our cherished notional liberties. The idea of man, the hunter, vigorous and independent, still has enormous mythical attraction for many people, even though the historical truth is probably just as likely to turn up woman, the gatherer, as the sustainer of the primitive clan.

We may have to make a new social contract for the whole earth before we can truly grant equal rights to the other animals but while we are moving towards this there are many gradual steps to be taken. Universal suffrage in Britain was a piecemeal affair and it's unlikely that this, in many ways even more radical, progression towards animal equality, will be any different. We can begin by admitting that their basic biological urge to live is our 'right to life' and that we no longer need a nice bit of meat for magical 'goodness'.

We must admit too that we have no innate 'right' to take away their lives unless we adopt the position of fundamental Judaeo-Christianity, the literal acceptance of the theology of a primitive farming community, as binding on human and non-human alike for all foreseeable time, with all that that entails. Our only rational justifications for such a right are that we do it because we can, which is an exercise of power; we do it because we want to, or because we have convinced ourselves that we must in order to promote the welfare of our own species.

19

None of these seems a particularly high-minded or ethical stance, and certainly doesn't constitute an ethic to justify the flood of pain, terror and death in which we daily engulf the rest of the animal kingdom. Finally and fully admitting that we are animals too and that our only truly human dimension lies in the exercise of our imaginative and conceptual abilities, we should be able first to understand the nature and magnitude of the suffering we inflict and secondly to move towards its end.

BULLOCKS

The bullocks have come to stand around us
where we sit after the climb between
the last of summer scabious, Tom Thumb
purple vetch and frilled bladderwrack
of campion flouncing the chalk track.

Hairy hobbledehoys, their coats are soft
still as children's skin. Castrati
who will never come to bullhood
they stare at us mildly. I try to probe
their promptings. Do they want us to speak?

Perhaps it's food they're after: the sacks
of hormone stuffed tasties the husbandman
I use the old word, scatters to keep
their eunuch flesh plump and tender. All boys
together, they have each other in this brief playground.

October's last lush lawn's their lunch counter.
Below, apart, those belles of the swung bag
their mothers brush the browse with tough titties
while the bullfather shoulders his beefcake
waiting alone for his day on, chafing.

Only these gentle lads take notice of us
twolegged interlopers in their workplace
turning out meat and dairy produce
from the green shopfloor. Our dog snaps them back
when curiosity brings them too close in.

Shoulder to shoulder they stand, not jostling.
We're encircled, almost faced down. I can't
look them in their bullseye. That one's galled
biblically. Some have tagged ears, tattoo numbers.
Will they overwinter? My prescience

hangs heavy as the bullish seedpods
or the cows' skin milk jugs. We get to our feet.
Below us the warm house is folded
in a bowl of hills. They stand back as we go
heads turning to snuff our scent, grave Bisto kids.

2   Life and Death on the Farm

Every year some 33 million cattle, sheep and pigs are slaughtered in the UK. For those who find such figures useful, that is roughly sixty a minute. These slaughterings are carried out in some 1,200 slaughterhouses and knackers' yards, licensed since the Slaughterhouses Act 1974 by the local authority. The Ministry of Agriculture, Fisheries and Food had no comprehensive list of these premises and was unable to give me their precise number. There is no adequate national or local government inspectorate and such inspecting as is done will tend to be under the Food and Drugs Act rather than the 1974 Slaughterhouse Act, and for purposes of hygiene rather than humanity.

Meat Technology by Frank Gerrard recommends a period of twenty-four to thirty-six hours of fasting for mature animals when they arrive at the slaughterhouse. For this they are kept in 'hunger or fasting pens' and given plenty of water. Animals which may be nervous or exhausted from a possibly long and certainly frightening journey make poor carcases. Their temperatures may rise, causing poor bleeding and the glycogen in the muscles may be used up, which will both affect the rate at which the meat sets, and encourage the spread of bacteria.

Hunger, the semi dark and a state of dull apprehension probably help to make most animals more docile when the time comes for them to be taken to the stunning pens or slaughter hall. Under the 1974 Act all animals except those killed 'by the Jewish method for the food of Jews' or 'by the Mohammedan method for the food of Mohammedans' must either be killed 'instantaneously by means of a mechanically-operated instrument in proper repair' or stunned and 'rendered insensible to pain until death supervenes'.

In practice stunning, not instant death, is the usual method because: 'Bleeding is most thorough when the heart and respiratory functions remain in action as long as possible.' (*A Textbook of Meat Hygiene* by Edelmann (revised by Mohler and Eichhorn). Stunning, and the next stage 'sticking', may only be done by licensed slaughtermen except in certain exceptional cases where 'by reason of an accident or other emergency the contravention was necessary for preventing physical injury or suffering to any person or animal'. Animals may be stunned by a captive bolt, the method preferred for cattle, or by an electric current passed through the brain. Pithing, which means inserting a cane, knife or metal spike into the base of the skull either to sever the spinal cord or destroy the medulla oblongata, would seem from the 1977 edition of *Meat Technology* to be still used, but its legality could, I think, be questioned under the Act since it does not employ 'a mechanically operated instrument'.

The insensible but still living animal is then usually strung up and 'stuck', although sticking sometimes takes place on the floor. The main blood vessels above the breastbone are severed and the animal bleeds to death. Stunned animals are of course in the same state as anaesthetized humans awaiting an operation. Left alone they will regain consciousness and in the case of stunning by an electric current recovery is very quick and quite complete. In Jewish or Mohammedan methods of ritual slaughter there is no preliminary stunning before the throat is cut. Unconsciousness comes with the draining of the blood from the brain and nerve centres. The removal of as much blood as possible inhibits the multiplication of bacteria and makes a more marketable carcass.

The total population of cattle, sheep and pigs in the UK in 1981 was just over 53 million. If over half of them are slaughtered every year the average life expectation of these animals is less than two years. It ranges from the few months of the veal calf, through the year of the meat pig to the four years of the ewe and the dairy cow. Most beef cattle are killed when they are between eighteen months and two years old. We have replaced the evolutionary concept of the fitness to survive with the fitness to die.

Natural selection weeds out principally the young and the weak. With our concentration on animals as food units we kill them, with the exception of veal calves, in their young prime, robbing them of many years of natural life. Left to themselves cattle could live about fifteen, sheep ten and pigs eleven years. We let them grow only to the human equivalent of late teenage and early motherhood.

The quality of the short life we allow them varies not only with the species and its needs but with fashions in farming and above all with the supposed economic laws of supply and demand. The urge to survive is so strong in all animals, including humans, that even the hardest and most joyless conditions can and will be endured. The fact that an animal survives is no real indication of its state of wretchedness as the opened gates of Belsen showed us. We animals will stay alive and even attempt to reproduce in accordance with our genetic imperatives. Calves grow in slatted pens, hens lay in cages, prisoners look for sexual relief and affection behind bars.

As well as the 33 million mammals killed each year there are at any given time some 58 million fowls and nearly 10 million assorted ducks, geese and turkeys being fattened for the table. In 1982 we spent over half our weekly food expenditure, 448 pence out of 809, on meat, fish and dairy products, including eggs, and by far the greater part of this, 254 pence, was on meat alone.

To produce it we set aside for grazing and the production of animal feed nearly 14 million hectares of agricultural land, as opposed to only 5 million for cereals, fruit and vegetables for direct human consumption. At the same time of course we produce butter mountains and milk lakes because of government, including EEC, schemes to help certain types of farming. I've said that farming and therefore the lives of millions of our fellow creatures are subject to fashion and economic law. This isn't new, of course. John Clare noted in the nineteenth century one of the periodical changes in agricultural habits. Stall tethered cattle began to be fattened on the new root crops which were grown on the recently enclosed commons. Both labourers and animals lost their common rights. Describing their vanished liberty he wrote:

> The sheep and cows were free to range as then
> Where change might prompt, nor felt the bonds of men.
> Cows went and came with every morn and night
> To the wild pastures as their common right;
> And sheep, unfolded with the rising sun,
> Heard the swains shout and felt their freedom won;
> While the glad shepherd traced their tracks along,
> Free as the lark and happy as her song.

The agribusiness has intensified seemingly in parallel with the human population explosion, each, I suspect, feeding the other. In the UK this intensification can be dated to the collapse of the yeomanry in the eighteenth century as fewer and richer landowners who had the capital for modern techniques of intensive farming, bought up the smaller men. Only the rich could afford to drain, invest in new crops and machinery and ship produce to the London market. Yeoman and husbandmen dwindled to labourers, losing the vote and their own homes in the process while animals no longer appeared differentiated in wills as 'my little brown gelding', or 'the black cow' but were lumped together as livestock.

Primitive farming, although it contained within itself the potential for factory farming, had preserved some relationship between farming humans and farmed beasts and indeed still can. It's this that attracts children in particular to the idea of the farm because it seems to promise a close relationship between us and them. The caring small farmer today who delivers his own lambs, retains this relationship but in a sense it is a blind that covers the true nature of what is happening.

As more and more people became town dwellers it was easier to obscure the developments that were taking place in farming as it was largely taken over, or put under the shadow of, the food producing industry. The separation between the countryman and the townee in some ways too makes even elementary change for the benefit of the animals more difficult since the countryman sees his way of life as misunderstood and threatened.

Factory farming as we now see it should never have been allowed to happen by those employed in the industry themselves. Unfortunately, however, farm workers have traditionally been overworked, underpaid and kept in a state of dependence by the tied cottage system. To protest at the building of a battery shed and organize your fellow workers to protest with you was to endanger both home and livelihood. At the same time, those who work on the land now tend by temperament and conviction to be more conservative and this has meant, ironically, accepting the change to factory farming because their employers have ordered it so.

The employers will often be either a distant syndicate to whom the figures that matter are those of financial profit and loss or conversely the shooting gentleman who is used to rearing game birds for slaughter. Hens in particular are by custom and speech thought mindless and silly. There is more than a hint of chauvinism at the root of the mass exploitation of laying hens in their metal harems, dropping their eggs and squabbling for room to stand up. Even debeaking which is advanced as an economic necessity has undertones of gagging the shrew or gossip. An element of contempt for the reproducing female may also be there and male chauvinism is still very strong among all classes of agricultural workers and landowners.

It could perhaps be argued that the phasing out of the wife's involvement in the family farm which Clare documents as taking place in his lifetime, accelerated and made easier the introduction of modern techniques. Historically, poultry and the care of young animals belonged with the farmer's wife. Removed from her mothering function it was easier to complete the necessary desensitization and see them merely as food units. The wife's function now, where she is involved at all, is usually on the secretarial and accounting side.

The process begun in the eighteenth century, which saw both the beginnings of protest and a deterioration in the lives of animals, and has accelerated with the constant improvement in farm machinery needing a smaller and smaller workforce. The 2.25 million workers who were left on the land after the great exodus of the late nineteenth-century agricultural depression have now dwindled to 712,000 (June 1981), half of whom are farmers, partners, directors and their husbands and wives who own nearly 73,000 holdings, with an average size of 646 acres. A freeholder in Elizabethan times often kept his family in comfort on twenty acres.

Farming has become the agribusiness, one of the most efficient in terms of per capital production in the country, but this has been achieved at a terrible cost to millions of living creatures. The evils of factory farming are now so widely known that it seems almost inconceivable that a democracy is unable to satisfy the very real public desire for reform. The latest NOP market research poll carried out before the General Election in June 1983 for GECCAP showed eighty-eight per cent of the people questioned were in favour of the reform of factory farming conditions. Forty per cent wanted battery egg production banned; seventy-five per cent wanted the export of live animals banned and seventy-seven per cent wanted ritual slaughter for religious purposes stopped.

Yet there are still some 45 million chickens, imprisoned four or five to a cage measuring sixteen by eighteen inches or eighteen by twenty inches. The average wing span of a chicken is thirty inches. Pigs and veal calves (although these have dropped by nearly a half since 1978) continue to be reared in small metal cages on concrete floors or in wooden stalls, in semi darkness and a solitary confinement only modified when the cages are stacked in tiers side by side. The public is frightened by the threat that changing these conditions would increase the price of food but even with this threat, and in time of recession when everyone is concerned for day-to-day housekeeping, ninety per cent of those questioned in the poll said that animals should be given sufficient freedom of movement to turn round, stretch their limbs and groom themselves, which would effectively mean banning the use of existing stalls, crates and cages.

The West German supreme court of appeal at Frankfurt has ruled that battery cages constitute cruelty under federal law because battery hens cannot exercise their basic behaviour patterns. In 1976 the Council of Europe made a convention that all farm livestock should be allowed these basic needs according to their species, a convention that the UK is now in theory bound to comply with. But the Council of Europe is notoriously lacking in teeth to force any compliance with its conventions. It is the EEC which can issue directives which must ultimately be obeyed. Accordingly, the West German decision was brought to the EEC on the grounds that if one member state was to introduce such a ban the others must too, in compliance with the Treaty of Rome's provisions for maintaining equality of competition among the members.

Such a ban, however, would require the consent of the very Agricultural Ministers who preside over factory farming in their own countries. Not surprisingly the question was referred to a committee and the present proposals are for cage sizes already the norm for the UK. Only Italian hens would be better off.

Yet such conditions aren't necessary even to intensive farming and may indeed be counter-productive in terms of the health of the animals. Dead or sick animals are useless to the farmer. Under pressure from public opinion systems are now being developed or re-examined which could phase out the cages very quickly. In essence they involve the keeping of animals in large sheds or covered yards in deep straw. There are several variations that can be made on this basic pattern. Although not as satisfactory as the free range system they could make an enormous improvement to the way of life of millions of animals.

They do, though, raise several political and ethical problems which deeply divide the animal rights movement. The goal of one wing is vegetarianism and ultimately veganism for everyone. It can be argued that to improve

29

existing conditions merely puts off the achievement of this end. Only by exciting public sympathy with the atrocities of factory farming, this argument runs, can society be moved towards an ideal position. To improve conditions without abolishing the meat and dairy product industry will lead to apathy and a feeling that things aren't so bad but that they can be endured for the sake of our health and our palate.

Politically the case for total abolition would be weakened. A new campaign would have to be begun on quite different lines. It would no longer be possible to appeal to humane revulsion against unnecessary suffering. Human greed would be implacably opposed to any acceptance that to kill is wrong in itself, whatever the quality of life of the living creature concerned.

On the other hand, there are those who argue that such a goal is unrealistic for the foreseeable future and that every chance to improve the day-to-day life of farm animals must be taken. This is the stance of Compassion in World Farming which strongly promotes the humane alternatives to the cage and pen.

If I ask myself the question which would I as a biological unit rather have: an improved life with an early but unforeseen death or, for my lifetime, a concentration camp existence, ending also in early death but with the hope that things might be completely changed for my great great grandchildren, if such there should be, I am quite certain I would accept the enhanced life. Nor do I believe I have the right to make a decision for other creatures that satisfies my moral scruples and long-term strategy at the expense of their day-to-day well-being. Those who do so must have adopted the root error of the exploiters: that is, not to apprehend other animals as individuals, each of whom will suffer in its own flesh, but as a mass, a species.

I can't believe that we should take on ourselves the right of generals to expend life and cause suffering in the short term for the sake of a possibly illusory victory. We have no mandate for this from the creatures we profess to speak for and in exercising such an authority we are simply exercising human dominion in a different hat.

Short of a climactic or man-made holocaust which destroys both men and other animals, vegetarianism as an international way of life will be brought about by a combination of pressures as, without a holocaust or bloody revolution, social change always is. These changes will be both ethical and economic. The history of women's suffrage and black emancipation shows that these two elements must work together. The temptation of idealists is to rely exclusively on the ethical aspect while the economists fall into the opposite error of claiming that all change is the result of economic rather than political or social pressure. According to this argument, votes for women were achieved not by suffragettes but by women munitions workers. Any dispassionate look at the question must surely see that both the theory and the economics for change are essential to provide the necessary dynamic. Neither will do it alone. Women worked in mines and factories for decades without being given a vote. The theoretical arguments have to be put tirelessly and the existing theoretical base changed before economic pressures can hope to bring forward the solution.

The theoretical basis of vegetarianism is an acknowledgement that all animals are equal in their right to live out their individual lifespan and that no other creature has the right to cut it short.

In practice carnivores have always lived their lives at the expense of others. Humans, however, are not exclusively carnivorous and have no need to be so in modern society. Indeed it could be argued that to take part in the meat-eating chain is culturally and aesthetically inappropriate to the age of the satellite and the space shuttle, certainly for Western industrialized societies.

Economically, the world's land would be better employed producing fruit, vegetables, cereals and vegetable protein for all, than in producing expensive meat products for richer nations. The world's politicians, too, would be better

31

employed in working out a rational distribution and financial structure, which got rid of the obscenity of babies with swollen bellies and stick limbs in Africa while European farmers were ploughing food back into the ground, than in haggling to keep up the price of their own national produce. There is still enough land to feed us all as vegetarians. If the world's human population goes on increasing it's the only way in which we can all be fed. Pouring vegetable products into animal processing units to convert to fleshly protein to be consumed by other animals is frankly uneconomic. Yet all the time we try to extend this archaic process, to turn more and more species into food units: deer, rabbits, kangaroo; anything which might be termed fit for human consumption is at risk. Not content even with our own domestic farm animals the agribusiness looks constantly for new ways to make money out of animal suffering and early death, taking in previously wild creatures, reaching down to farm the sea bed not only for its vegetable but for its animal life.

Several arguments are of course advanced against universal vegetarianism and I will try to deal with the most common. There's no answer to the simple uncaring greed of the 'Why shouldn't I?' kind. If carnivores recognize no imperatives apart from their own desires, and justify their actions simply on the grounds that humans can do what they like because they are top dog, there is very little that can be said in reply. You might as well try to argue a wild tiger out of its dinner.

One argument that's often put forward is to ask what would happen if we all became vegetarians tomorrow. In this country the answer is quite simple. The 53 million farm animals would be taken off the equivalent of death row and given the right to live their lives to the point where the quality of that life through age or illness wasn't worth continuing with. Instead of promoting fertility and constant reproduction as we do now we would use contraception and abortion, as we do for ourselves, to control their population.

Advances in genetics, which make it possible to grow a human foetus 'in vitro' and reimplant it in a carrier mother, to determine sex before birth and, it's now claimed by Japanese scientists, to distinguish which sperm will produce male and which female offspring, would be used to limit the number of males, unwanted except for their meat. In the first few years or even decades, 'support an animal' schemes run by animal welfare societies could provide compensation to farmers for allowing the animals to live out their lives. We would have the pleasure of seeing creatures browsing in the fields without the threat of their deaths constantly sullying our response to them, and yet be spared the shock of an empty countryside.

Alternatively we could offer them, if not a total reprieve, a first stage towards it of statutorily increased life expectation to, for example, middle age. The immediate result for the consumer would be that meat would become a rarity and that the nutritional gap would have to be filled by non-meat versions of traditional foods made from vegetable protein, the kind of things that are already commonplace in health food shops: proto-veg, soyamix sausages, burgers and so on. An immediate impetus would be given to the development of a vegetarian food industry and the amount of money channelled into it would ensure the necessary consumer research to improve the taste and quality. So much convenience food is now eaten that such a transition would be far less difficult than at any time in the past. Farmers would be encouraged by subsidy either from national or EEC funds to convert to growing sources of vegetable protein.

Compassion in World Farming estimates that if battery hens were uncaged and distributed among existing farms the average flock would be about two hundred. Many more people if given the chance to rescue them might like to return to the backyard hens of my childhood, though with a changed attitude that allowed them a much longer lifespan and didn't mark them down for the pot as soon as they stopped laying. They would live out their six to eight years instead of two or three, which is all even the lucky free range bird can expect now.

The price of eggs would probably rise, at least in the first year or so. I say 'probably' because it's impossible to be sure

33

until the experiment is made. At the moment the farming industry is able to mount a powerful propaganda campaign every time a change in the way we eat and produce our food is suggested. By threatening increased prices they are able to frighten the public out of its humane desire to see factory farming at least severely modified if not abolished. Yet even among the ranks of farmers themselves there is disagreement about what is economically feasible. It is, for example, much more common now to see hillsides in light soil areas covered with half circle tin huts for free range pigs, like some porcine housing estate. Farmers who rear their pigs in this way have clearly decided that there are economic benefits as well as ethical ones in the shape of healthier animals. Yet others remain unconvinced even by reports on this by fellow farmers and continue with their factory line.

This disparity underlines the need for a proper collation of evidence, followed by a determination of policy by the government. However much voluntary agencies may exhort and produce leaflets, their effect is always limited by their acknowledged bias. It should be the Ministry of Agriculture, Fisheries and Food that investigates the whole question of factory farming which polls have shown to be of deep concern to the public, and then either legislates to improve conditions or offers subsidy incentives to farmers if legislation is felt to be too much like state interference.

I have no doubt that a properly conducted study would highlight the benefits of deep litter and free range farming. To bring about such a study and then see its results put into practice, either by incentives or law, should be a priority with the animal rights movement. The Ministry of Agriculture, Fisheries and Food hasn't as yet been properly pressurized. It adopts a non-interventionist stance which shows itself in the fact that although the Minister has powers of entry into slaughterhouses and knackers' yards under the 1974 Act, the MAFF had no list of these premises, nor even an accurate total of them, which its handful of veterinary officers are supposed to inspect.

Many animal rights activists will criticize the gradualist approach which I am suggesting as a thought-out long-term strategy. I believe that it is the only one that has a real chance of success, and which doesn't put us in the morally dicey position of expending, by refusing to improve, the lives of other creatures who can't give their assent.

One problem for the animal welfare movement is the number of areas of concern and suffering. Where everything needs to be done it's hard to plan a campaign. It's hard, too, when there is disagreement about the desired goal. I believe that it must be universal vegetarianism, in the sense that no animal must be made to suffer or be deprived of its natural lifespan for our culinary or nutritional convenience. I believe, too, that this must include all creatures that have a central nervous system and are capable of feeling pain. Chicken and fish aren't for me acceptable elements in a vegetarian diet, much as I would like to deceive myself in the case of fish. Just because our sympathies aren't aroused by cold, scaly creatures who live in another element it doesn't mean we have the right to kill them. In the event that the long awaited ET turned out to be a highly technological flounder we should have no more right to kill him or put him in a laboratory than if he resembled a dissident Russian scientist.

An acceptance of this goal, even if seen as a distant prospect, would make it easier to plan a strategy of movement towards it and to work out the graduated steps forward. Crucial to its achievement is a continual growth in personal, as the complement to public, vegetarianism. Becoming a vegetarian is much like giving up smoking. It has many of the same pressures to overcome and may induce similar withdrawal symptoms of craving for the lost palliative.

Many people give up eating meat for a time and then, as smokers do, gradually slip back. Some find it easier to phase it out slowly, others to cut it off at once. I believe that any reduction in the amount of flesh eaten, and therefore ultimately of animals reared for killing, is good in itself and I don't believe that long standing vegetarians should look down on backsliding or partial vegetarians. What matters isn't our own purity but the number of lives saved now from the factory farm and eventual slaughter.

If you are someone who was once vegetarian and have somehow let it slip, don't feel the kind of guilt that can lead to a mixture of aggression and apathy. Begin again. If you feel you must have some meat for health reasons (hepatitis for example can bring on a craving for animal protein) you can still exercise choice in avoiding factory farmed products. If your sympathy can't extend to fish and fowl at least avoid the mammals.

Social pressure on vegetarians, although much less than it was because of the recent emphasis on health foods and the dangers of a too fatty and bland diet, is still very daunting for many. I find that the chief problem is eating out in someone else's house. Restaurants can usually provide an omelet or a salad, and Chinese, Indian and Italian restaurants usually give the vegetarian a tasty choice among their indigenous dishes. Invitations to lunch and dinner or supper at home I respond to with a cheerful announcement of my position and an offer to withdraw or eat just the vegetables. This usually results in the cook being provoked into preparing a non-meat dish which is the envy of the rest of the table. Airlines should always be notified about inflight meals in advance. Vegetarians often do better than the consumers of plastic ham.

Many people eventually move on from vegetarianism to veganism which involves rejecting all products which exploit other animals for human use. This leads to another problem: will there be lactating cows and laying hens in the ideal animal democracy? I am quite clear in my own mind that eating any form of egg, as long as the animal that produces it is able to pursue life, liberty and happiness, is for me morally acceptable, and I would include in this, undeveloped foetal organisms of all kinds, for example frog spawn and plankton.

At present the chicken, by and large, lives and dies appallingly. The rearing of table birds and their death by the mechanical knife is intolerable. Birds are particularly susceptible to fear, probably as part of the defence mechanism that makes them able to launch into instant flight, yet they are strung up by their feet on a conveyor belt still conscious and struggling and drawn towards the electrical stunner and the mechanical knife. The MAFF after constant complaints about the brutal transport, unloading and deaths of poultry asked its advisory council (FAWC) to report on the whole process, which it did in January 1982. The council found that the birds' treatment when being hung on the shackles line was 'sometimes unnecessarily rough', that large numbers were not stunned before slaughter and that when the automatic throat cutter failed, for any of a variety of reasons, to make a proper cut, some birds 'enter the scald tank before they are dead'. Their conclusion was: '. . . the view is widely held that the nature of the slaughterhouse operations, their high degree of mechanization and their speed and scale result in sentient creatures being treated with indifference. We have much sympathy with such views.'

However, even these criticisms from their own advisory council have produced only a recommendation by the MAFF for a voluntary code of practice. Such codes are always a relief to the *status quo* party in any conflict of interests since they mean business as before with only a few cosmetic touches. Unfortunately, only legislation or cash incentives produce real change.

The dairy cow and her calf pose greater problems. We certainly don't need as much milk and its products, cheese and butter, as we now get. Nor do we need to induce other cultures to switch to our fashion for feeding babies on reconstituted milk to use up some of our surplus. We only do them a disservice.

At the moment we produce this surplus by inducing ten monthly lactations, following pregnancies which result in veal calves and replacements for beef and dairy herds. This presents, I think, a real moral dilemma rather than the straight choice which it's often made out to be. Milking a cow, goat or ewe isn't in itself likely to cause suffering, unless it's done roughly, and indeed it may be beneficial. Cows go on needing to be milked long after calves can be weaned. Here they are very like humans, who can and in some cultures and at some periods have suckled their young for up to three years, or chosen to wean them much earlier.

I see no reason why we shouldn't use the milk of other animals if we can do it without causing suffering and death, and indeed, insofar as milk and its artefacts supplement a meatless diet, such use may actually help to improve the lot of all animals. It can't be beyond our capacity with the help of modern genetics to devise a management scheme that would allow us to have milk, and replacement dairy calves sufficient for our needs. The old cow would be allowed to live out a much longer life in even the initial stages of the new method, serving as nurse cow to calves that had been removed from their mothers early to give as little sense of loss as possible. Cows would be allowed to keep a calf from time to time or serve as nurse cows to fulfil their need for motherhood, a state so important to most female mammals.

If, though, no such humane scheme can be devised I can see no alternative to complete veganism, using dairy substitutes. I would rather that the cattle species vanished altogether, except perhaps for a few kept in nature parks, than that the present level of suffering and death should continue, simply to preserve a species as a biological curiosity or so that our eyes can be gratified by a landscape with cows.

The same kind of revised management will have to be applied to sheep and goats, giving them fewer pregnancies and consequent lactations and an extended lifespan. If these conditions had the force of either law or subsidy a few years would teach us how to manage them for the greater good of all.

The public has, as the previously quoted poll shows, come a long way towards rejection of the doctrine of cheap meat at any price in animal suffering but a new campaign is needed to begin to change its collective thinking on the question of life expectation. If a cow may live to fifteen, we should and must query the morality of cutting her life off at four or five, the equivalent in human terms of twenty-five, when she might have many more years of life which could even be seen as useful to humans.

What is needed is a reversal by the general public, and in particular by the agribusiness, of our usual way of looking at farm animals; that is, for us to begin to see them not from our, but from their, point of view. Since they can't sit round a table in negotiation we have to represent imaginatively their concerns in any debate. Perhaps what we need is a ministry or department of animal interests or rights which would automatically oversee and have a voice in any legislation or practice which concerned non-human animals, a kind of animal ombudsman. The theoretical starting point in any discussion for such a representative would be the ideal way of life as conceived by the animal itself, if it were capable of conceptual thought instead of reacting instinctively to immediate circumstances as we judge, at this state of our knowledge, that most non-human animals do most of the time.

From the beginning, discussion would therefore be between two equal points of view which would have to reach a compromise. A statement of animal rights such as that which emerged from the RSPCA's symposium at Cambridge in 1977 would be a basis for the ombudsman's primary position. The important new element would be that the case would be presented for the first time from the position of an equal partner to a contract. In any such discussion the animal rights representatives would need not only a set of principles but the research which would provide the data to argue for them. Too much is still assumed about animal reactions and needs. Their inability to speak precisely leaves us to observe and conclude. Because we ourselves rely heavily on speech for communication we are particularly bad at interpreting other non-verbal forms.

This shows itself strongly in our treatment of animals for slaughter, which I believe should be a major and early battle in a gradualist campaign for animal rights. If an animal is to be killed it should be moved as short a distance as possible. Death should come to it. Slaughtermen recognize the stress that transporting animals produces by giving them a period of recovery in the fasting pens before slaughter. So intense is this suffering in terms of fear and strain that it's reflected in the very tissues of the beast and can contaminate its carcase. Yet few have argued from this that such a degree of misery in the lead up to death must be wrong in itself.

At one time death came to the farm, as for example in the annual pig killing, and it at least came swiftly. The growth of the human population and consequently of the animal one to feed it led to animals being transported to large abattoirs that could deal out death on a massive scale. Twelve hundred slaughterhouses processing 33 million mammals a year means an average of 27,000 for each premises or nearly a hundred each working day. The simple callousness that killing on such a scale must necessarily bring to those who do it, if they are to be able to carry out the job at all, also works backwards to affect the journey towards death.

From the moment that the animals leave their home farm they are psychologically deadstock. It's obvious that the longer the journey the greater the fear and stress. After the great cattle drives in America the animals needed several weeks' recovery in quiet grazing before they were fit to kill. Yet not only do we send animals to local slaughterhouses to be killed, we even export them abroad, in spite of attempts both in this country and by EEC directives to end this practice.

However short the journey, though, I believe it is too long. Just because non-humans don't use speech for communication, their fear at being transported is, I believe, even greater than that of a human because they can't be reassured or given any palliative explanation. Even for many pets, being transported is a frightening experience, especially at first. Dogs and cats may learn that it isn't, unless their destination is always the vet's surgery, have an unpleasant outcome and grow to enjoy it. The wretched animal on its way to slaughter has no such experience. It's locked into its fear by lack of communication, among strangers, jolted and uncomfortable at the very least, and unable to exercise its instinct for flight or the human alternative to flight, of hope. If most animals have no apprehension of the future then they can't hope but simply suffer, shut in the present, even more fiercely perhaps than a human would.

Once again the system needs to be reversed so that in the matter of their death, it is their viewpoint that should be considered not, as at present, automatically, the human one. Few of us are eager to die and most of us are agreed that we should like it to happen as quickly as possible and in a familiar non-frightening setting. We should like, too, to die with as much dignity and as little interference as possible. I believe that if they could articulate them these would be the instinctual requirements of other animals as well.

With a terrible irony some of the most horrific animal deaths take place at the demand of religion. Ritual slaughter is built into the Slaughterhouse Act of 1974 and into the EEC directive on the subject and it is certainly on the increase in this country in spite of the overwhelming opposition to it of the British public, seventy-seven per cent in the National Opinion Poll for GECCAP in Spring 1983. Big business has moved in to slaughter ritually, according to Mohammedan rite, thousands of animals for export. Without pre-stunning the animal's throat is cut and it is left to bleed to death. Here is a clear case for the animal ombudsman. Such practices should be illegal under British law. If religious groups object to not being allowed to kill as inhumanely as they wish they have the options of importing meat or, better still, becoming vegetarians, which isn't prohibited by the Jewish or Muslim law.

It is peculiarly offensive that large sums of money can be made out of what is quite simply torturing animals to death under the guise of religion. The European Directive 74/577 (1974) permits 'national provisions related to special methods of slaughter which are required for particular religious rites'. This means that section 36(3) of the UK Slaughterhouses Act which permits ritual slaughter without pre-stunning could be amended with the EEC's blessing. A private member's bill could achieve this, even without an animal ombudsman, and it is implicit in the demands of GECCAP. It is perhaps the first and minimal step to be taken on the long march to freeing the farm animals.

LEMONCHIC

Laika forgotten
little bitch star
sometimes in the night
it worries me that
I can't remember
whether you are still there
orbiting among the other debris
a perpetual epitaph
pinpricked out of black tissue
skypaper of our
impatience and pride
that couldn't wait
but sent you tracking down
eternity
warped to your coffin
as surely as kittens
bound in a drowning sack
or if answering the whistle
of a pressed button
you became shot star
homing into ash.

We played God with you
Zeused you like Ganymede
but not out of love.
Did you think you were being punished
Callisto perhaps, for those seconds
only when your nosing dreams
beguiled you from duty
beyond the school walls
flirting your rump like ordinary dogs
not put down for headlines?
At the time they said
you were trained for it
as if we could take
obedience for assent
silence for unsuffering.

I make your small bones
this constellation for all those
who can't say no.

3 A Living Death

The same arguments which apply on either side of the farming debate also apply to the problem of vivisection: do we or don't we have the right to inflict suffering and death on other sentient creatures for the benefit of our own species, and what degree of suffering is acceptable or necessary? The vivisection debate is, however, given an extra bitter twist by the irony of the two basic assumptions that it is only relevant to use other animals for research because humans are themselves a sub-division of the animal world, and yet we are sufficiently unlike the rest to have created and be able to use this position of power.

The extreme form of this dual perception of likeness and unlikeness precedes Darwin's exposition of evolutionary theory. It's implicit in the practices and beliefs of the early vivisectors whose systematic establishment of vivisection as a tool of medical research Richard Ryder has documented in *Victims of Science*. Given the immense influence of Descartes, it's not surprising that the systemization of vivisection should have taken place in Paris. It demonstrates, I think, how important it is constantly to attack the theoretical base of any system we wish to change.

Descartes believed that an animal's cry of pain was a mechanical response to stimulus and not an indication of thought or feeling. It must be remembered that vivisection, like most operations on humans at that time, was carried out without anaesthetic of any kind. François Magendie (1783–1855), professor of medicine at the Collège de France and his successor and pupil Claude Barnard (1813–78) carried out thousands of dissections in this way, often in public.

'Twice did the dog, all bloody and mutilated, escape from

his implacable knife and twice did I see him put his forepaws around Magendie's neck and lick his face.' (*British Medical Journal*, 22 August 1863, p. 215.)

It's some comfort that Ryder is also able to document that there was protest and disgust at the growing practice and it's good for a writer to be able to number Dr Johnson among the public protesters. Nevertheless, the growth of vivisection seems to have been unstoppable, almost like a deliberately cultivated tumour.

Human life was itself cheap. Life expectation was low. The standard of living for the rich and middle classes improved but for the mass of the working class it was declining steadily with the drift to towns and the increasing pace of industrialization. The slave trade, too, was at its height. The concept of hierarchy reinforced the acceptability of vivisection. White labourers were known not to have the same sensibilities as their more cultivated employers and the conditions of their lives in the late eighteenth and early nineteenth centuries certainly brutalized many of them. Yet below them were black slaves who could be thought of as inhabiting some borderline of sensitivity between the white poor and the organ grinder's monkey. Non-humans, on this scale, must suffer least, hardly indeed at all.

Thus vivisection became established during a time of great suffering for both human and other animals, yet whereas many of the brutalities and inequalities that were acceptable then have now disappeared, the laboratory animal is still part of our late twentieth-century society. The discovery and widespread use of anaesthetics has given a new weapon to the vivisectors who can allege that no actual suffering takes place since the animal subjected to surgery is usually insensible and is killed if it is in pain when consciousness returns. This in theory puts it in the same position as an animal being fattened for slaughter. Laboratory animals are well fed and housed because they must be healthy to be of any use. Then they are, in effect, stunned and stuck. If we accept that way of life and death for our convenience in the case of farm animals we should logically accept it for animals as research tools for our benefit. Anti-vivisectors who aren't also vegetarians will be forced to argue on other grounds of necessity and efficacy, that is, in the vivisectors' own terms and using their language and available data.

Fortunately, as I've said before, humans aren't always consistent or rational in their views and reactions, and many people in Britain are able to go on enjoying their Sunday joint while being appalled by much of the use of animals for laboratory research. In the interests of the millions of animals experimented on every year (4,344,843 in 1981 in Britain, according to Home Office statistics) this is good, even though it's based on a dangerous illogicality. Neither meat eating nor animal experiment are necessary to directly sustain life. Both are accepted because they suit most of us.

Vivisection for 'medical research' is justified once again by a resort to fear. As we are afraid that without meat some vital component of diet will be missing and we shall become ill, weak, impotent or merely cranky, so we are afraid that without medical research we or our loved ones will become incurably ill or die. This is a simple animal instinct for our survival, and that of our offspring, given the superstructure of the human imagination and the attendant resources of modern technology.

The medical profession still maintains a traditional veil of secrecy over its doings, and laboratories are closed to the general public. The feeling that we, the public, don't understand is still deliberately fostered by individual doctors and the profession as a whole, both in our own treatment and in the overall development of medicine. Those who want to know what is going on must rely either on snippets of journalism, which are often garbled or presented too briefly to be of any real value, or must search the medical journals and deduce the true nature and methods of any piece of research from the careful tissue of jargon in which it's embedded.

Faced with this barrier which is designed to calm its fears, the public, as repeated opinion polls have shown, is nevertheless uneasy about many aspects of the use of animals in research. While many people are prepared to accept a limited use for true medical purposes, the waste of thousands of animals in the testing of cosmetics, weapons and household products is unacceptable. Once again there's a certain useful illogicality in this division into what we see as necessary and unnecessary. Strictly, if we admit the possibility of using other sentient creatures' suffering and death for our own benefit, this should apply equally to making sure that a new food additive isn't cancer inducing or a new cosmetic or detergent won't burn the skin. Products which are freely available and apparently innocent of any capacity to harm may conceal health hazards as bad, or indeed the same, as those being treated by drugs and surgery, especially since they may fall into the hands of children. Every home is full of lethal substances which can kill or injure.

The two uses of vivisection which seem to me morally unambiguous even if one admits the use of animals for medical purposes, are research into tobacco and its substitutes where no one who smokes can any longer be in any doubt about the hazards, and the testing of weapons. Mankind has a long history of involving animals in its warfare, particularly the horse, but it does seem peculiarly obscene to irradiate, infect and tear living creatures without even the excuse of immediate self-protection, in preparation for something that should never happen. Once again the concept of hierarchy is at work. If you are contemplating, even if only on paper, the death of millions of your own species the actual deaths of lesser creatures seems permissible to the military mind. They are merely more counters in the war game.

However, as with the phasing out of factory farming and the spread of partial vegetarianism, I believe that anti-vivisectionists must exploit such illogicalities as part of the constant attempt to save lives. If the public out of puritanism and a psychological ambivalence about 'painted women' is prepared to reject the testing of cosmetics on animals this should be welcomed.

Similarly, if the rejection of animal research in testing food additives contains an element of distaste for the whole idea of increased consumption of junk and doctored foods, and a desire to return to more 'natural' eating habits, anti-vivisectionists should welcome and use this attitude no matter how little foundation it may, under examination, prove to have as a nutritional fact. In the same way the fashion for health foods, with the consequent fall in the consumption of meat and dairy products, must be encouraged by true vegetarians, even though it may turn out to be just a passing fancy. Every area of vivisection should, I believe, be subjected to as much attack in the form of moral pressure and a continual bombardment of facts, pictures and publicity as the anti-vivisection movement can manage, even though some of the arguments presented may fall short of total abolition, and may use such reactions as public squeamishness or puritanism.

The key to abolition, however, must lie with medical research and there are two ways of responding to this, neither of which rules out the other. There is first of all the simple ethical ground which applies to all our treatment of other animals: that we have no right to bring about their suffering and death simply because we can.

Laboratory animals are either bred for the purpose, live out entirely unnatural lives and die unnatural deaths or they are brought in after a period in the wild or in the home as pets or on the farm. If they belong to the second category they will have additional suffering in the loss of freedom and their way of life and the terror of new and hygienic man-made surroundings. Even humans who understand more or less what's happening and why they are there, feel disorientated, helpless and frightened in a hospital because they are no longer in control of their own lives and bodies. Other creatures, who haven't even given a half assent, will feel these sensations, I suspect, far more strongly.

At best the animal can be said to live, before it's actually used for experiment, a half life, caged, often fed on nothing more interesting than water and compressed food pellets, away from natural light and air, like any other battery reared creature except that in addition the atmosphere it breathes must be clinically germ free. For creatures who still retain a highly developed sense of smell the very air of a research institution may contain more stimulus to fear and give a greater degree of sensory deprivation than we can imagine.

The day must come when even this twilight life which, as Richard Ryder points out, may make them 'so crazed or inert that they are no longer representative examples of animal life' (*Victims of Science*, p. 88), is exchanged for the positive horror of the research programme the animal is intended for. Even the simplest research will inflict fear and discomfort. Humans know how painful and distressing just an injection can be, and we, unlike most other animals, have soft penetrable skins. Substances may be injected into or withdrawn from the body, including of course the very anaesthetics that are meant to dull further pain.

Anyone who has ever taken an animal to the vet knows the trauma it suffers, and this is when it's accompanied by someone it trusts, and at the hands of a skilled vet whose livelihood depends on curing the patient while causing it as little pain and stress as possible. Those who handle laboratory animals are not usually trained or experienced vets. They may not even be qualified medical practitioners but students or laboratory technicians. It isn't necessary for them to be wilfully sadistic to cause pain and terror. Simple incompetence, haste or inexperience will do. Many animals have, even at the vet's, to be forcibly restrained before their liberty is invaded by the needle or thermometer. Unless the animal has been made inert by the conditions of its life it will be inclined to resist as a natural instinct, except for those creatures like rabbits, whose reaction to a predator is often passivity, or dogs whom we have taught since mesolithic times to obey and help us.

From this point on there is a Dantesque descending spiral of suffering ending in a death which, as Ryder points out, may be far from painless or instantaneous and once again administered by the incompetent or the inexperienced. The length of experimental life may be quite long in terms of misery although not of course seen against an animal's natural life expectation. Draized rabbits and smoking beagles, electroded cats and monkeys may be strapped or locked into their experimental situation for weeks or even months.

The anti-vivisector who takes the view that we have no right to inflict suffering and death on other creatures even for the benefit of our own species has no difficulty in rejecting outright the animal concentration camps which the testing and research laboratories are, for animals will be used at both the discovery and the proving stages of any new drug or product as well as, for example, behavioural research which has no immediate human application.

Such an argument however won't weigh with most of the medical profession, the Research Defence Society, the breeders, testers and international drug companies who are in it for the fat profits, or much of the general public fearful for its health and life. Other reasons for phasing out vivisection must be found if it is to be finally abolished. It's an indication of the progress that has been made by the constant efforts of anit-vivisectors in the past, often in the face of ridicule and abuse, that even the Medical Research Council now pays lip service in a negative way to this ideal in a letter of 9 December 1982 to the National Anti-Vivisection Society.

In the Medical Research Council's Establishment Code all their staff, and I quote, 'are particularly asked to use, *wherever possible*, procedures which do not involve animals ... *Regrettably* there is no chance that in the foreseeable future the use of live animals for research and similar purposes (much of which is for the benefit of animals as well as humans) can be dispensed with' (my italics).

The section which is in parentheses in the last sentence shows a typical example of muddled thinking on this issue. It implies that to vivisect perfectly healthy living creatures is all right if it does good not to humans but to non-humans.

In the first place most animals now exist either for the benefit of humans or, at least, are allowed to go on existing because their lives in some way benefit us. Anything that doesn't is labelled vermin and may be shot, hunted, snared, poisoned or gassed. Protected species, which largely consist of those endangered in some way by us, are protected not for their but for our benefit, because we don't want to lose something which may please us by its curiosity or beauty or remove a possibility of pleasure from our environment.

Research which is said to be of benefit to other animals will almost certainly be in an agricultural, domestic or zoo context. The notorious example of letting a transparent panel into a herbivore's stomach to study the digestive process would presumably come under this heading of benefitting animals.

Secondly if, evolutionarily speaking, each species exists for self-propagation, only the suffering of a member of that species leading to benefits for that species could logically or morally have even a spurious validity. In evolutionary terms a mouse may not suffer for a cow, at least not in the mouse's view of its own genetic survival. No ethical justification can be found for the pain of a mammal which is no use to man except as an experimental subject, in order to convey supposed benefits to mammals which we use as food machines. Nor have we any evidence to suggest that the smaller the animal the less the suffering. Pygmies and giants among humans may differ in their responses to pain but not because of body size.

A laboratory mouse or rat isn't necessarily 'lower' in evolutionary terms than a cow or indeed a dog. Even researchers attest to the intelligence of the rat. We use them partly because they are traditionally regarded as vermin and partly because they are easy, quick and therefore cheap to breed. They can be produced in great quantity, in germ-free conditions and as close to replicates as possible even without cloning. This makes them both practically and psychologically (to us) perfect instruments for research.

There may be said to be even less justification for causing pain let alone death to one non-human animal for the supposed benefit of another, precisely because it can't comprehend what is happening to it or why. Humans can be appealed to by reason and altruism to offer themselves for the good of others, even for non-humans, and the conviction that they are doing the right thing may even lessen suffering, but no such palliative is available to the laboratory animal which suffers, like the animal in transport to the slaughter-house, in blind and hopeless incomprehension.

The Medical Research Council's letter does however reflect a growing awareness and distaste for the use of animals in experiments. I have said that it pays lip service to the ideal of abolition because it was written in answer to a plea that more money should be spent on investigating alternatives to live animals. The NAVS has quite rightly identified a key problem: that, because of human fears, no real progress will be made until it can be proved that the use of non-human animals is not only unethical but also unnecessary, either because the results obtained are suspect and unsatisfactory or because there's a better way, using alternative testing techniques.

The very existence of these techniques raises the historical question of vivisection. Pro-vivisectionists point constantly to the real discoveries of benefit to humans that have been made using live animals for research and production; insulin and the Salk polio vaccine are two notable examples. The argument runs that these wouldn't have been possible without vivisection, therefore although perhaps regrettable, it is still necessary.

To argue that because something was discovered in one way it wouldn't, couldn't have been found in any other is clearly false. Yet this is the backbone of the vivisectionist argument. It stretches back into the past and forward into the future causing money to be poured into, for example, cancer research of which a great part consists of growing in healthy mice and rats tumours of a different nature from those which are specific to humans, and denies resources to alternative studies which depart from the *status quo* of testing on animals.

Magendie and his followers initiated a method of research which has, like a great cuckoo, shoved aside all others. It undoubtedly appeals to the sadist in some vivisectors, the kind of cold, childish sadism of the latency period which causes pre-pubescents to pull wings off flies and keep animals like frogs, newts and beetles, not for their own beauty but out of quasi-scientific curiosity. It requires exactly that stifling of imagination and empathy that Shakespeare characterized as hardening of the heart.

Ryder quotes several comments on this by scientists in their evidence to the Royal Commission of Enquiry which was appointed in 1875.

' . . . vivisection has special and distinctive liabilities and amenabilities to abuse; for it does act on our emotiono-motor nature in a particular way', Professor George Rolleston (Linacre Professor of Anatomy and Physiology at Oxford).

'The continual sight of animals being acted upon, particularly if the observer has any enthusiasm for the pursuit, in a very short time blinds the man's sense of humanity', Dr John Anthony.

Anthony had worked in Paris and seen the horrific practices there. English scientists were quick to blame the French for going too far and for showing so little concern for the living creatures under the scalpel. The Royal Commission was impressed by the evidence but in the way of such bodies looked for a compromise which was of doubtful logicality: vivisection shouldn't be banned entirely because it sometimes brought benefits to human kind and a unilateral ban in the UK would cause scientists to emigrate, which wouldn't benefit the animals. This last argument is only too familiar in many controversial areas.

The result was the Cruelty to Animals Act, 1876, which has never been superseded in over a century of growing abuse of animals. It licensed vivisectors and gave them protection from prosecution under other animal welfare legislation. In 1981 sixteen licensees were admitted to have been reported for infringing the Act but no action was taken against them because 'the circumstances were not considered to justify such action' (letter from the Home Office of 27 September 1982 to the NAVS, cited above). Not surprisingly 'the circumstances' haven't been disclosed for general discussion of whether or not they did warrant prosecution. The fact is that no licensed researcher is ever prosecuted as a result of Home Office inspection and with fifteen inspectors to police the fates of 4.25 million animals this is only to be expected.

The total number of experiments rose rapidly after the passing of the 1876 Act, from 270 in 1878, to 4,679 in 1895, to nearly 38,000 by 1905. The rise coincides with the rise in the human population and consequent conditions of poverty, with chronic malnutrition and overcrowding which earlier in the century had resulted in epidemics of typhoid and other hygiene-related diseases, and of tuberculosis and other diseases of the lungs. It also coincided with the expansion of the patent medicine industry and the development of vaccines and serums as the poor, in particular, tried desperately for cures to ills which really needed prevention.

In evolutionary terms we had created a situation in which many of us should have died, and only the fittest survived; that is, a classic case of species over population, endangering the food and territory resources that in other species would have resulted in some form of lemming-like reduction in numbers. With our ability to outwit the basic evolutionary principles, however, we were able to continue to increase our population even in the face of the spiralling demands such increase brought, mainly by legislation to improve public health by every means from education through free school milk to public baths and drainage schemes.

Nevertheless, the concept of human life as fragile remained and life expectation was low (it had risen to 32.9 by 1890) until the great improvement in conditions brought about ironically by the Second World War. Tuberculosis is an interesting indicator of such developments. Deaths from the disease had fallen steadily as living conditions improved, and continued to fall in spite of the depression, between the two world wars. It can probably never now be proved whether streptomycin, the build-up of natural immunity or rationing with its balanced diet contributed more to the final conquest of what had been known as 'the white man's scourge', yet, even so, streptomycin is one of the drugs whose development owes nothing to animal research. (For a detailed list of such discoveries see *Clinical Medical Discoveries* by M. B. Bayly, 1961.)

From my own family history, which included five deaths

from TB in my mother's generation, I can document the money spent on patent medicines which it was hoped would cure or at least strengthen the sufferers in their struggle against the disease. The figures for animals used in research under licence for this period make interesting reading.

During the First World War the figures actually fell as money and effort was concentrated on treating the wounded who in themselves provided medical evidence and advances of benefit to humankind in peacetime. Few people would argue from this that wars should be encouraged.

The numbers of animal experiments declined from roughly 95,000 in 1910 to 70,000 in 1920. However, they had leapt again to over 450,000 by 1930, doubled by 1939 and nearly again by 1950 to almost 2 million. Ten years later it was 3.75 million and the figure reached what must be hoped was its peak in 1971 with over 5.5 million or one animal for every ten humans in the UK. The decline by a million since then is undoubtedly the result of public unease brought about by constant campaigning by anti-vivisectionists and by the introduction on however limited a scale of alternatives, coupled with the economic recession.

The greatest increase in the use of animals for research came then after the Second World War with the expansion of the consumer society. Significantly, the proportion for medical research fell from sixty-two per cent in 1920 to thirty-two per cent in 1972. (Incidentally, none of these figures includes animals used for the production of sera and vaccines since this isn't research and therefore doesn't need to be licensed.) During this period the human death rate has stayed almost stationary at a real figure of 650,000 a year, a decrease of roughly six per cent of the population on the figure for 1900 but a similar percentage increase since 1930. The real gains have been in decreased infant mortality, giving a much higher life expectation, and the banishment of TB and fever epidemics. Heart disease and cancer remain the two great killers in spite of the millions of pounds and lives expended in research.

The chief purpose of much recent testing has been to try to protect us, in theory at any rate, from killing ourselves with new products. Medical research confers by transference a kind of pseudo-scientific respectability to the testing of hundreds of new synthetics produced all the time. In marketing them, the manufacturers rely heavily on an element of ascertainable fact as part of their propaganda to persuade us that we need a new shampoo or washing powder. It must be alleged that it will convey 'real' benefit and in modern terminology that means something which can be tested and shown. At the same time the companies are anxious to avoid unfavourable reports and reactions from the public, with the consequent possibility of insurance claims.

Testing drugs to be prescribed for medical purposes, which is required by law in this and other countries, doesn't automatically of course confer immunity from insurance claims as the Thalidomide and Opren cases have shown, and it's hard to see in the light of this why, for example, cosmetic firms continue with what is an increasingly unpopular practice unless it's a form of self-censorship. Do they abandon the development of a shampoo containing some new substance that will make human hair shine or be more 'manageable' if lengthy tests on rabbits' eyes, the so-called Draize test, show it to be an irritant? Because of the fear of industrial espionage and the constant battle for the public's purse, secrecy surrounds all such research and development, and this extends to any discussion of the reasons for continuing to use animal testing in areas where it would seem to be counter-productive with a public increasingly hostile to it. The desire to get ahead of rivals in a particular market seems to outweigh all other considerations.

Many consumers would query whether we need the constant refinement of everyday products. Ironically, revulsion against what is seen as the artificiality of modern life leads to the development and marketing of more 'natural' goods, suggesting a nostalgia for 'older country ways' that exist only in the Golden Age mythology humans are constantly reinventing. We are locked in a self-perpetuating pattern. Once created, large companies, like living organisms, must fight for their own survival, and the thousands of workers dependent on them must support their continuing battle in the market place. This is equally true whether their product is for cleaning sinks or dosing humans and other animals yet there's this difference, that only in the case of medicines and dangerous substances is testing on animals required by law (the Medicines Act, 1968). All other testing is voluntary, except for the animals. In 1981 testing not required by legislation involved 1,432,305 experiments or thirty-three per cent of the annual total.

The largest single figure was 1,695,381 experiments for the 'selection of potential medical, dental or veterinary products or appliances'. This is the group which should give greatest health concern to the general public, and it's by extrapolation from this that the testing of other substances which I've already discussed takes its colour. It involves not only the experimental research itself but the notorious LD50 test where a variety of species are dosed with the substance orally, intravenously, or by inhalation until half of the experimental group are dead. The over half a million tests for acute and chronic toxicity presumably fall into this section.

Sometimes the figures are hard to explain. Although nearly 1,700,000 experiments were required by law for the selection of medical, dental or veterinary products, a further 700,000 were licensed in this category, not required by law, making it the single largest group, or half the annual total. It's in just this area, however, that the greatest doubts are beginning to show themselves about the validity of the whole exercise. Crudely, we test drugs and medicines on other animals, just as the Queen of *Cymbeline* wished to do, to see if it will kill them. If it doesn't, it might not kill us. If it makes them better it might make us better. We do it because they are alive in a sense which we can see and understand, and in which we know we are too, and because like us they might die or become very ill.

Such testing belongs to the era of ignorance. We now know, or should know, that all animals aren't alike and that what induces a particular effect in one species will possibly produce a quite different one in another. Thalidomide is the tragic, classic case and I don't need to describe it in detail here; it's enough to say that after further extensive testing the laboratory rat, staple of all animal experimentation, appears to be completely immune to its malforming properties. That great stand-by of modern medicine, penicillin, however is poisonous to guinea pigs.

These are two extreme examples at either end of the testing scale. Between lies a whole spectrum of varying doubt. Inter-species testing is a blunt instrument which can only produce hit and miss results because of the infinite variations between species in the five stages through which any substance is processed by the body: absorption into the bloodstream, distribution, mechanism of action, metabolism (speed and pattern of transformation) and finally excretion. These vary even between one human and another. A drug which causes headache and nausea in one person may show no side effects in someone else or may kill as in the case of Opren.

The crude practice of extrapolating from non-human to human which Magendie systematized has blinded us to the differences between species with the one great universal that we all live and die. It has led us to neglect that proper study of mankind in this field, as in so many others, which is man. It can't now of course be proved, but it is perfectly possible that our present state of knowledge would be greatly advanced if we had never set off down the vivisecting road, if not a single non-human animal had ever been experimented on but if we had taken from the beginning a way of concentrating on the observation and treatment of humans, adding the technological advances of tissue culture, gas chromatography, radioactive isotope labelling and so on as they became available.

We are locked into a position where multinational companies with turnovers of billions control the drug industry in all its stages. According to a recent report in the *Guardian* (Andrew Veitch, 29 March 1983) the National Health Service bill alone is about £2 billion. The Department of Health allows them to make a minimum twenty-five per cent profit on the capital they employ to research, develop and market their drugs. The British taxpayer is therefore directly subsidizing animal testing by private companies. At the same time such research is kept in the companies' own hands and can be done behind closed doors. Alternative methods such as patient follow-up and surveillance to gauge the true effects on humans would begin to open up the closed world which they operate by involving not only patients but GPs in a more democratic system of assessment.

Animal testing is an easily controlled and secret process. Animals after all can't talk. Not only can they give nothing away, neither can they detail the side effects which humans often find such a disturbing aspect of new drugs. The companies, except when things go badly wrong, are eager to maintain the *status quo*, including the aura of power and inaccessibility that surrounds them. Human fears and the traditional air of Hippocratic mystery help to confirm their position. Recent medical historians (*The People's Health 1830–1910* by F. B. Smith, 1979) have noted the shift in emphasis from the nineteenth-century concern with community medicine which achieved drastic reductions in mortality, to the present concentration on individual treatment which is heavily dependent on drugs and surgery, both of which have involved massive research using live animals in the tradition of Magendie.

The apex of this development is the current obsession with cancer research and transplant techniques, especially for the heart. Some physicians have already expressed concern at the amount of money being spent on these operations which of their nature can only benefit a limited number of people. There is an appalling ambiguity in waiting for one human, usually a young fit one with several decades of life expectation, to be killed in a road accident to provide a new heart for another, ailing and often aging. The introduction of compulsory seat belts and crash helmets, which can be seen as a form of preventive community medicine, it must be hoped will drastically reduce the supply of replacement hearts and perhaps redirect attention to preventing heart disease with a fresh look at diet and living conditions. In an ideal world in which people weren't killed on the roads, and humans died after a full lifespan there would be few, if any, usable hearts. It seems therefore even more short-sighted to base a school of medicine on what we hope will be a temporary phase. The development of transplant techniques used 14,553 animals in 1981, including 335 dogs and twenty-four primates.

Perhaps the greatest manipulation of the public by fear is in the field of cancer research. Partly because of the recession of tuberculosis, cancer has become the dominant disease of our time in the collective imagination. Increased longevity adds to this impression because we must all die sometime of something. Nevertheless, the discovery that smoking is carcinogenic in many people hasn't stopped smoking overnight although there has been an encouraging increase in the number of those with the strength of will to give it up.

The companies and the public through the charities pour money into cancer research in the hope of a miracle drug that will be sovereign for every kind of cancer, rather like the mediaeval attempts to discover the philosopher's stone that would transmute any base metal to gold. There is a killing to be made by the first company to get there and from time to time the media erupt with the latest wonder cure, keeping the public in a state of expectation for something that may well never happen. Streptomycin is a misleading parallel here.

In 1981 just over 49,000 animals, including twenty-two of our genetic cousins, the primates, and bizarrely over 3,500 birds, fish and reptiles were subjected to 'intentional induction of neoplasia'; that is, they were 'given' some form of cancer. Among them were 45,000 mice and rats, whose tumours are commonly sarcomas while those of humans are usually carcinomas, but in whom tumours can be speedily grown for treatment and study. The very artificiality of the exercise can be gravely misleading. C. J. Williams in the *British Medical Journal* for 27 March 1982 commenting on the great hopes raised by immunotherapy which 'worked in experimental tumours in animals', went on: 'Sadly these hopes were largely disappointed . . . Indeed even while these studies were starting warning voices were suggesting that data from research on animals could not be used to develop a treatment for human tumours.'

There are of course enough human tumours to provide a great quantity of research material. Faced with cancer, many patients would volunteer to be, as we so graphically call them, guinea pigs out of altruism, which the other animals can't be asked to exercise on our behalf, or in the desperate search for a personal cure. As long ago as 1972 the former Chief Scientific Adviser to HM Government, Lord Zuckerman, pointed out in *The Times* of 26 October that an increase in funds for cancer research could not be effectively used and indeed could 'encourage mediocrity and the routine pursuit of ideas which may long since have ceased to be fertile'. What is still needed is a new approach based on prevention, and on human studies from the whole patient to the minute complexities of genetic material.

Nearly 100,000 more animals were used for carcinogenecity screening of new products in 1981. Of these over 50,000 were mice whose short lives, even when they are allowed to live them out to the full, bear no relation at all to the human lifespan and therefore to the time which a human may be exposed to a cancer-inducing agent. Such testing may be positively harmful because it can divert attention from possible long-term effects. Yet clearly no company is going to waste ten years testing a product. The short-term test is a blind that gives a false sense of security to the public. By the time the real effects of any product become apparent in humans the company which marketed it may well no longer exist.

Perhaps one of the most dubious areas of so-called 'medical' research is that of behavioural studies and the induction of stress. Here again it's hard to see what useful extrapolation from non-human to human there can be since we are so clearly not the same. The gross over-simplification that must result from inflicting stress and suffering on inarticulate non-humans can surely teach very little worth knowing about humans, and if it's intended to illuminate the reactions of non-humans, enough of them already live in stressful conditions and can provide a mass of everyday data. In 1981 over 62,000 animals were involved in such experiments, including the use of 'aversive stimuli, electrical or other' for the sinister category of 'behavioural training', and in research which interfered with the central nervous system.

Once again the proper research tool, if the object is to learn about human behaviour, is the human volunteer. It will be objected that you can't remove or destroy bits of the brains of such human volunteers. However there are people already damaged by illness or accident who would gladly co-operate in a research project and would be able to provide far more valuable information about the human mind than the endless shocking, depriving or fitting with electrodes on thousands of rats, cats and monkeys can ever do.

The truth is that human volunteers must be treated with respect, even almost as equals. The researcher can't play God with them. The research must be precise, painstaking and painless. Once again the use of non-human animals seems not only a very blunt instrument but an easy option. Often the results obtained could already be predicted by common sense and experience. Ryder cites a piece of research reported in the *Journal for Experimental Psychology*, no. 22 1970, in which a number of rats were given inescapable electric shocks to test the theory that high levels of fear reduce exploratory behaviour. The result was 'subsequent avoidance of the environment in which the shocks had been given', a conclusion whose only purpose must have been to be published so that the researcher should appear in print to further his career.

If vivisection research is to be allowed as an interim measure to continue, a panel consisting of at least fifty per cent lay people and including the animals' minister or ombudsman or his personal representative should be set up by the Home Office to consider whether any given piece of research involving live animals is really necessary. This itself should be seen as forming part of the phasing-out process. The Medical Research Council has already admitted that the use of live animals is 'regrettable'. The next stage is to systematically reduce the numbers used. It isn't premises or vivisectors who should be licensed but each experiment, after the closest possible consideration of what is intended and involved. At the moment a licence gives the holder complete freedom as long as he isn't detected infringing the largely bureaucratic rules by one of the fifteen inspectors who are supposed to oversee the nearly 4.5 million experiments.

Such a validation panel would put the onus on a researcher to prove that his research was necessary and didn't duplicate existing work. It would be part of the panel's remit to ask for specialist advice in any field and to suggest alternatives to the use of live creatures. It could for example refuse to permit LD50 test for non-medical research, and supervise the numbers of animals used in any agreed test. Many companies would find that a statement that no animals had suffered in the production of the substance whether for cosmetic or household use would actually enhance sales.

The chief opposition to an overseeing panel would, I suspect, come from the military rather than the medical profession and it may well happen, in spite of the public's distaste for the testing of weapons on animals, that this will be the last area to be civilized. It epitomizes the entrenched attitudes and vested interests that have to be overcome in attempting to abolish vivisection. Many millions are invested in the production of weapons. As I've remarked earlier, those who are contemplating the destruction of humans in their thousands will certainly see non-humans as expendable cannon fodder and all the arguments about national security will be advanced both for continuing to experiment on non-humans and for keeping the nature and extent of such experiments in cloak and dagger secrecy.

Nevertheless, as with the movement towards universal

vegetarianism I believe a systematic gradualist approach is the only one that will ultimately succeed with vivisection too. It will have the added benefit that lives of humans as well as non-humans will be saved and suffering lessened as we progress, however slowly, towards the goal of total abolition.

SONG OF IGNORANCE

Ding dong bell
Pussy's gone to hell
brought in a plastic bag
as though already dead
one fifteen you pay
to have her put away.
Who put her in?
The landlord rich and grim.
You can't keep a pet
take it to the vet.
Cruel to be kind
you won't leave her behind.
Can't just let her roam
I tried to find a home.
At least he doesn't cry
a hypocrite's goodbye.

Ding dong bell
hell's a basket cell
waiting for the gas
to make your terror pass.
Moggy black and white
howling in your fright
we are not so brave
I too dread the grave
when my spark like yours
flickers and expires.
Vivid in the sun
your days used to run
dodged the flying wheels
and the winter chills
now your nine threads snap
no escape from that.
Though your one life too
is unique to you
you must cease to be
when we turn the key.
Imagination fails
for animals with tails.
The species we preserve
but not the single dove
poison gulls as pests

so terns can have their nests
and thousands die
to titillate our eye.

Who'll pull her out?
The vet in white coat.
O shade of William Blake
for this tamed tyger's sake
you ring the bell
For Pussy gone to hell.
Ding dong bell
deep and dark the well.

4   Life and Death Together

Man's oldest friend seems to be the dog. There's archae-
ological evidence from the bones at camp sites that we have
lived together since mesolithic times. Without embarking on
a Just So story it's still interesting to speculate about how
our cohabitation first came to pass. For it to have lasted,
both parties to the contract must have got something from
it. Man could have driven dog away or dog could have left
at any time.

I suspect that the first dogs were brought back as puppies,
perhaps even for food, and that some escaped the pot or
rather the roasting spit, became imprinted by the twolegged pack leader and attached themselves to new packs of
human hunter gatherers. There were several ways in which
dogs could have been useful to humans from the beginning,
as guard, retriever, hunter and eventually herder. In return
there was warmth, food and a place to shelter.

The essential nature of our interdependence and the
things we do for each other has changed remarkably little,
even though a dog's duties nowadays may range from
guiding the blind, searching for drugs, controlling crowds of
humans or other animals or providing a reason to get up for
thousands of lonely people each morning, a function it
shares with millions of other pets.

The pet populations of cats and dogs in this country are
estimated by Pedigree Pet Foods who make surveys for
marketing purposes at roughly 5.5 million dogs and 5
million cats. Cats are on the increase; dogs slightly on the
decline. Apart from these homely animals there is a large
inestimable population of feral cats and some dogs.

To look after the health of all these and other animals

there are just over 2,000 private veterinary practices and three main charitable organizations: the Blue Cross, the PDSA and the RSPCA. Then there are a number of small, often localized animal welfare societies including the Cat Protection League, the various sanctuaries and local rescue groups.

In spite of all this, the RSPCA estimates that some five to six hundred thousand dogs and even more cats are destroyed every year because they are unwanted. Many of these can be described as physically or mentally unfit yet a proportion of them, probably about five per cent in the case of dogs, are completely healthy animals, and in others the unfitness may be simply a tendency to roam or the first signs of old age which make them unattractive to potential new owners.

There is therefore an enormous ambiguity in our attitude to, and treatment of, our pets. On the one hand we have millions of them and spend even more millions on them; on the other the wastage rate runs at between twelve and twenty per cent a year. This figure is a guesstimate arrived at by taking the total population for pet dogs and the replacement rate of puppies, and giving the dog an average lifespan of ten years. Because so many people and organizations have the function of destroying unwanted animals it's impossible to arrive at a true figure which would have to include some calculation of the animal's age. The dog licence which in theory might provide information is so largely ignored as to be statistically useless.

Humans seem to be the only animals that keep pets, although there are, of course, inter-species relationships of mutual benefit. Birds perch on mammals to remove ticks and parasites, a small fish will take up with a larger one for protection and crumbs of food. Primates in research institutes will adopt the human pet-keeping attribute. Lucy, the first signing chimpanzee, had a pet cat. Her relationship to it seems to have been part maternal part sibling.

Leaving out the use of other animals as cheap and specialized labour it looks as if our obvious need for pets, especially in an urban industrial society, must have very deep roots. Recent research suggests that humans who keep pets get real physical benefits from the relationship, so much so that they even recover more quickly from heart attacks. We seem to need both to give and receive extra-species affection, probably because our own human relationships are full of stress and demand.

In most human societies people touch each other in a context which, whether consciously or unconsciously, is usually sexual. Yet we must, in common with the other primates, have somewhere in our pre- or early hominid ancestry the practice of mutual grooming, and indeed there are traces of this in different societies and on various occasions. Sometimes it has been the custom for women to groom men, or men to groom each other or even, at the hairdresser's for example, for men to groom women, but certainly nowadays these are the exception. Only in very close relationships, sexual or parental, do we break the individual envelope of physical privacy that surrounds each of us, and those who for some reason don't accept this are likely to find themselves misunderstood through confusing the usual signals.

The English are notoriously or traditionally undemonstrative and this may lie at the root of our equally traditional responsiveness to other animals. We feel safe with them and in control of the relationship. We can pick them up and put them down at need. Other animals can be banished from the room; their demands, except for food, can be resisted until we need to respond. We don't have to maintain a constant sexual wariness with them as, because of the unseasonal nature of human sexuality, we must with our peers.

English women, in particular, traditionally find relationships with dogs, horses, cats and even birds more restful and easy to manage than those with other humans, especially men, because of this. But it isn't just a female response. Men experience similar difficulties both with each other and with women, difficulties which surface in the kind of emotional cop-out disguised by sayings like: 'A man's best friend is his dog', with its implicit put-down of human relationships. Even when there is no overt or primary sexual element present, humans are often territorially aggressive. This takes a social form in the constant struggle to upgrade our surroundings or status, whether at home or at work, both in comparison with peers or with the dreamworld of television or magazine advertising. The combination of sexual and status wariness and the constant need to exercise our verbal skills in communication make most of our relationships uneasy in every sense.

Pets don't compete with us although we may compete with each other in our choice of pet. The whole pedigree industry depends on this. They will, however, compete flatteringly with each other for our attention. In return they give us the opportunity to exercise both a restful dominion and our primate urge to groom by stroking, and by grooming itself, without evoking erotic responses that we either don't want or can't deal with. It would be silly to pretend that there's no erotic content, on both sides, in our intimate dealings with other animals although ours is largely unconscious or repressed. Dogs, cats and horses and even imprinted geese can be aroused by humans and quite often are, but even the weakest, most timid owner remains in control and is under no real threat but perhaps benefits by the mild, governable titillation.

There are of course people who feel no need of pets, as some humans feel no need for children. I haven't touched upon the pet as child substitute because it's so well known as to be a cliché. There's one sharp difference that should be mentioned, though: pets don't perpetuate, they don't confer immortality and on the face of it there can be no genetic basis for our nurturing of them, which is perhaps why other species have hosts and parasites but not pets. Our care for them is an entirely human extrapolation from parental, sexual and social drives, rather than a straight substitution. It is, rather, a displacement of emotions secondary to the physiological and genetic drive to reproduce, the nurturing that tries to ensure the survival of our own young.

Some people, and they are also to be found in the animal rights movement, believe it's positively wrong to own pets, that it is a form of exploitation in itself and yet another and therefore unacceptable form of man's dominion. They would argue that we have no right in this, as in any other interface where human and non-human meet, to use and impose our will on others. There are, I think, two inescapable facts that conflict with this view. First, the world is inhabited by a myriad species of creatures interlinked in Teilhard de Chardin's biosphere. Secondly, man has, by weight of numbers and development, covered the whole planet in a habitation network so that apart from a very few remaining wildernesses (and even these are crossed by an invisible aerial trackway at least), there is nowhere where human and non-human aren't forced to live together. We have in a sense domesticated the whole earth and even those animals who live in wild life parks and conservation areas are there on our sufferance, in some degree our outdoor pets.

To attempt to deny the extension of this network into our homes seems to me not only artificial but also potentially harmful to other animals since it would remove the meeting point, the front line as it were, of understanding and intimacy which is necessary if we are to improve the condition of all animals, especially those domesticated in laboratories and farms. To push back this front line out of our daily lives and homes would make it psychologically harder for most humans to empathize with other species. Pets are an invaluable bridge between us and them. Without them and without the intimate knowledge that living with them brings it would be much easier for us to go on seeing the rest of the animal world as completely other.

Curiously I think, pets, in particular dogs and cats and probably horses, have been insufficiently studied from a behavioural point of view. It's perhaps because it's more glamorous and attractive of research grants to pursue wild populations of dogs and cats in distant and dangerous places, than to observe those in the home who will be said to have been corrupted by human contact. The laboratory animal is thought to provide purer data for these reasons too.

Yet if the avowed aim of such study is a knowledge of ourselves it would seem that those closest to us might provide the most just reflection of mankind and our complexity. The ability to adapt, which is part of the evolutionary survival kit, makes it possible for other species to adopt a quasi-human existence. This existence seems to me, insofar as it is comfortable, as valid in itself and as a subject of study as that of animals in the so-called wild state. From an evolutionary point of view there is nothing sacrosanct about 'wildness'. It is merely a historical moment in the development of a species which we happen to be in a position to observe.

'Wild' has come to mean uncorrupted by human influence and is really a reflection, as a concept, of our own unease about ourselves. Both wild and domesticated dogs and cats have to make adaptations to survive in their environment. Neither adaptation is more valid than the other, yet the fear of being considered anthropomorphic in their judgements causes researchers to ignore the most obvious sources of information immediately to hand in the experiences of pets and their owners. It also makes it doubly difficult to solve what is perhaps the most interesting problem of all: the nature of animal perception. With all the implanting of electrodes in brains and the destruction of different parts of them, we still know almost nothing about how the non-human perceives itself and the world. In this respect we are as primitive as Descartes who concluded that animals don't feel because he had dissected animal brains and failed to find the seat of feeling or imagination.

Yet a real understanding of how the minds of other mammals work could be of immense value both to us and to them. We know for example, any pet owner knows, that like us both cats and dogs dream. Does this mean that they have a rudimentary imagination? We know, too, that chimpanzees and other primates can recognize themselves and others both in pictures and in reflections. What does this mean in terms of the nature of a sense of identity and of the self, and is such a question and the hypothetical answer not just as valuable as counting the number of females serviced by one silverback gorilla male?

Literature in particular testifies to our continual involvement with pet animals, on whom we have projected our fantasies and needs for centuries. However, perhaps the time has come to abandon both the word and the concept 'pet' which has become almost a pejorative, implying a creature spoiled at the expense of deserving humans in order to gratify a selfish, usually silly and female, owner. Few pets today are really pampered out of all proportion to what we ask of them in terms of companionship, guarding and in the education of our children to be kind and responsible.

Such pets have in some ways replaced the old extended families which included servants, in particular nannies and companions. The main differences are that we don't pay our pets except in board, and instead of sacking them when they no longer give satisfaction or our circumstances change, we have the power to dispose of them finally.

They are in reality working animals just as much as horses who live out, or guide and police dogs. Just as some people query our right to keep pets so they also question our right to employ animals at all. It smacks too much of the slave populations of sub-humans in science fiction and seems like merely another aspect of mankind's dominion and exploitation.

Unfortunately, however, unless the other animals are integrated into human society they will disappear and we shall be left alone with only fading memories of our true place in the biological network. Though the other animals would no longer suffer since they wouldn't be born, such a state would, I believe, be psychologically bad for humans. We need the other inhabitants of our planet for many reasons but not least we need them to remind us of what it means to be an animal, rather as the Roman emperors at their crowning had to be reminded that they were still human.

We mustn't be afraid to make them truly part of our society or rather perhaps to conceive of a society in which we all have rights and duties. In the wild state an animal's duty is to sustain itself and its family when it has one. This gives it a purpose which although not consciously expressed is understood in rather the same way in which we presuppose that we have free will by the very nature of our lives, even though we may not intellectually accept the concept any more.

When we take animals into our care we largely, except for the mousing cat, remove their innate purpose. Yet the drive to fulfil that purpose remains and we can give it an outlet in various work substitutes of use to us. This seems to me probably not only good, but necessary for the animal's well-being, even though I realize I may be accused of foisting the puritan work ethic on to those who didn't invent it.

Clearly any work that we ask non-humans to do should cause them no suffering or stress although it might be possible to make out a case for parity with humans, for example that the sufferings of pit ponies were no worse than those of women and children in the mines. Against this it can be said that humans, in theory, have the freedom not to take on a particularly hard or unpleasant job. Economic necessity, however, can remove or severely restrict this apparent freedom.

All the work that animals do must be without their initial assent, something which humans under all circumstances, unless for example they are in a slave population or the normal laws are suspended as in wartime, take for granted. Non-humans can only refuse by non co-operation: refusing a fence, not returning home, failing to learn what their masters dictate whether it's house training or searching for drugs. Failure to learn is usually diagnosed as stupidity when it may be simply refusal. When we do decide that an animal isn't co-operating then we may call it vicious or even mentally unfit. We want obedience from our domestic servants.

Nevertheless, pets do often maintain a degree of independence similar to that of such servants within a framework of seeming submission, and they may even become as tyrannical as house servants in their demands for food, attention and comfort. Yet the ultimate power of life and death is always ours and the figures of annual destruction reflect this. In 1982 the RSPCA found new homes for 101,981 unwanted pets but was obliged to destroy 102,857, a figure which excludes dogs and cats too sick or injured to live. Animals which withdraw their consent to work by a kind of passive resistance may well find themselves in this group and are already labelled unsatisfactory.

Using animals as unpaid labour not only raises the question of whether such use can ever be justified but also how far we can use them to substitute for humans, often in morally ambiguous or dangerous situations. Dogs and horses in police work are just such a long established yet dubious practice. There is something inherently distasteful in making other species into tools, for example as extensions of the police for crowd control and it would, I believe, be deeply resented in this country. Sensing this the authorities are beginning to develop other methods of crowd control but it isn't so long since one of the customary practices of protestors was to scatter marbles to cause police horses to stumble when they were ridden into crowds. Animals these days have to be non-combatant.

The public also feels uneasy about the rumours that circulate from time to time that governments through the military are training other species, usually dolphins and chimpanzees, for use in war. It seems a corruption of that very intelligence that makes them suitable for such work to involve them in our conflicts. There is a fine line between using dogs for example to take messages or sniff out drugs and using trained apes to plant explosives. It's significant, I think, that in war films it's always the villains who have tracker dogs, straining and snarling on the leash, for hunting down the heroes.

Public unease in this area also spills over into the testing of weapons on animals to make it doubly unacceptable, not simply as vivisection but because it seems morally wrong to make animals suffer in the propagation of something we regard as at best an evil necessity. We feel that humans must accept the responsibility and suffering attendant on war and not offload it on to other creatures, now that horses are no longer an intrinsic part of the war machine.

The horse still works, of course, but in this country its work is in the entertainment and leisure fields. Again such work confronts us with a moral dilemma. Many horses like to run and they seem to enjoy a sense of excitement, on occasion. Should we exploit and encourage this and how far? How can we be sure that only those who want to, take part in racing or polo, for example? Is it always true that something you don't like you won't be good at, that a horse that doesn't enjoy racing will show it by never winning?

A simple ban on the use of the whip and spurs might quickly sort out those who like it from those who, like most of us, can be flogged into it. Steeplechasing on the other hand should be abolished. It is dangerous to both human and non-human and is a piece of nostalgic harking back, a formalization of the chase that we shouldn't encourage in a civilized society.

Once again any attempts at reform must take on a multimillion pound and international industry, and one in which there has always been a strong link with the recognized criminal world. It would probably be foolhardy and self-defeating to try to get racing of both dogs and horses abolished completely within the foreseeable future but they can be made subject to most stringent controls, and the right to dispose of animals no longer wanted by killing them must be increasingly questioned and changed.

There's a severe legal problem here in that animals are seen as property and as such can be disposed of by the owner like any other goods. Yet there are already restrictions on what we may do with our living sentient chattels. We may not ill-treat them. Why then can we give them the ultimate ill-treatment of death without at least a vet's certificate recommending euthanasia? At the moment, anyone may kill an animal except where it is to be killed in a licensed slaughterhouse by a licensed slaughterman. I can shoot, fish or trap, and a recent television programme showed me how to kill a chicken and a rabbit, using live, until killed, animals for the demonstration.

Abolition of the automatic right to kill would of course be opposed by hunters of all kinds and would be far-reaching in its effect. Mousetraps would become things of the past except as used by council pest controllers. Once again as with all questions of improving the lives and prospects of other animals we run up against the limits to such improvements set by a society which is carnivorous. Nevertheless, the attempt has to be constantly made to push forward the boundaries of acceptability.

One stage could be the expansion of the existing dog-licensing scheme to include cats and the different representatives of the horse species. Licences would have to be taken out at birth and would pass at sale or transfer of an animal like a car registration. No licensed animal could be put to death without a veterinary certificate for humane euthanasia of a sick animal.

Such a scheme would encourage the spread of spaying and neutering and the prevention of unwanted births. People buying or acquiring animals would acquire a responsibility that couldn't be shrugged off by a convenient destruction. Obviously the scheme would work best if it were allied to an identification system and probably a painless tattoo as soon after birth as possible is the best method available at the moment, even though it smacks of the concentration camp and the surgical ward.

If licensed animals are no longer allowed to be killed at the wish of their owners without good medical reason, both the homing and sanctuary services provided by the different welfare organizations will need to be expanded. As with the adoption of children, advertising the needs of specific animals may have to become the norm. More money will be needed to pay for this and a proportion of it should come from those industries which gain by the existence of licensed animals, whether the pet food industry or the Tote. If they can't perceive that it's in their interests at least on the level of public relations to be seen to contribute to such welfare schemes, a levy system should be devised and put into operation.

In such a context it should hardly need saying that anyone convicted of ill-treating an animal, whether licensed or not, shouldn't be allowed to own one for at least ten years after conviction, if ever. It seems almost unbelievable that there should have been 1,508 convictions for cruelty in

77

1982. By far the greatest number, 1,048, were for cruelty to cats, dogs and horses, with dogs the highest at 761. The encouraging aspect of these figures is that only twenty-one juveniles were found guilty of cruelty, a halving of the previous year's figure. Cruelty to animals is now an adult rather than a youthful phenomenon and it may be that television has contributed to an improvement in the attitudes of children with its emphasis on the importance of pets and their care, in children's programmes like *Blue Peter*.

Thirty of the adult offences were serious enough to receive a term of imprisonment either enforced or suspended and there were 375 disqualifications from keeping an animal, all but nine for dogs which seem to be the easiest to neglect and ill-treat, probably because of the very closeness of our relationship to them. The majority of convictions for cruelty in this country arise not from carelessness or indifference, as for example in the transport of animals, for which there were fifty-one convictions, but are positive and deliberate acts, even when the deliberateness is in failing to restrain an impulse to violence or in prolonged neglect.

Against the sheer size of the numbers of animals ill-treated in battery and laboratory, what may be called personal cruelty, even if the number of prosecutions is only a percentage of the true figure of animal abuse, is mercifully small. There will always, in all probability, be people who will ill-treat those in their power whether human infants, prisoners, or the mentally ill and old, or non-humans, and we should try constantly to supervise and control this area of animal–human relations, yet the overall impression from the RSPCA statistics, apart from the figure for abandonment, is one of individual care in contrast with the institutionalized cruelties of vivisection and factory farming. The immense amount of voluntary work done in this field bears this out.

Much of this is carried on by women and this leads to a downgrading of it, even by RSPCA officers who may see themselves very much as the rational professionals paid to do a job as distinct from the amateurs who do it out of concern, which can easily be represented as sentimentality. There is, for example, even in the excellent *Report of the Working Party on Feral Cats 1977–81* a condescending tone in the presentation of a hypothetical case 'Stable and cared for colony', managed by Miss 'A' who is twice referred to as 'this single lady' in an illustration less than half a page long.

All of us have our own motives, largely unconscious, for what we do, including the choice of job, where there is an opportunity to exercise choice. Women are traditionally the nurturers and their education and the image of themselves they are encouraged to form reinforces this. They are expected to be practical rather than theorists and to involve their emotions in their work as least to the extent of taking on service jobs as teachers, nurses, secretaries, librarians. These are seen as projections from caring for their own children.

It's hardly surprising, then, that these reactions and needs will be present in many childless women and won't disappear even if they have never been exercised in bringing up a family. Women also live longer than men and may quite simply have years to fill without an opportunity any more to exercise those skills society and nature have combined to develop in them.

The stock caricature of an 'animal lover' as an aging spinster with her pussies serves vivisectors and factory farmers as a useful propaganda weapon. The dispassionate common sense (sic) attitude is projected as both masculine and scientific. The lack of progress in animal rights as distinct from the efforts of decades in welfare has stemmed, I believe, from the projection of these two images of opposed female sentimentality and male rationality. The very real progress now must owe something to an upgrading of women's attitudes and spheres of activity generally and to the desire among men, especially younger men, for an opportunity to express the more feminine side of their personalities and to conform less to the old male stereotypes.

Nevertheless, these two attitudes persist. Because of the way our society is organized, as an overall pattern it's women who care for animals and men who mistreat them, whether in the slaughterhouse, the military research establishment or the medical school. I find no pleasure in this observation and for the sake of us all, human and non-human, I wish it weren't so. I make it here because of the far-reaching effects it has had in the development of the animal rights movement, which has taken place against the background of other liberation movements and largely because of the involvement of a whole spectrum of mostly young men who have been necessary to give it sexual respectability and therefore credibility. The work of Peter Singer and Richard Ryder has been not only practically but psychologically crucial, not just because of their job status but because of their sex.

They have provided an acceptable theoretical base for this stage of the movement. I believe that the time has come, however, for a further development in the recognition of non-human animals as individuals which means grasping the problems of so-called sentimentality and anthropomorphism. This isn't of course to suggest that Ryder and Singer deny the individuality of non-humans, simply to recognize that their emphasis has necessarily been different.

The question of individuality, even in humans who can communicate with all the subtleties of speech, is a complex one. We exist as biological units with an appreciation of ourselves as different from others. As humans we know the precise historical moment at which we stand with its attendant past and future. Most of us know at least one of our parents, if not natural, fostering. This knowledge helps to define our individual self even though we may be a bundle of interacting mental parts rather than a single directing entity.

Non-humans have a foreshortened appreciation of past and future. A dog or cat, as pet owners know, can distinguish between the lengths of time of absence and show it by degrees of intensity in greeting. A chimpanzee will hide food or toys from its companions, lead them from the hiding place and return later to enjoy the treasure when the coast is clear. Similarly, carnivorous animals will come back for another meal from a concealed kill. Laboratory animals can be easily trained to remember which buttons to press for food or to avoid pain. Short-term memory seems common to most of us but, without speech, long-term memory may be largely inaccessible except in dreams and as a series of visual images.

The differences between human and non-human in the perception of themselves as 'I', the unique biological unit, seem to be of degree rather than kind; indeed, the very limitations of a non-human's perception of the outside world to primary sense data may intensify the feelings both of oneness and otherness.

In order to go on killing and eating and using for experiment we have to deny this sense of uniqueness to other animals and see them as somehow interchangeable within their species, as flocks, herds and batches. The pet owner's experience contradicts this, certainly with cats, dogs and horses. One will not do instead of another, except in the sense that parents who lose a child usually have another one as soon as possible to absorb the sense of loss, or unplaced emotions. It's only when animals are seen as food or research units that their identities become submerged. They are interchangeable in this context just as human slave populations have been when they were seen as so many units of labour.

To admit the individuality of non-humans is to bring them dangerously close to us. It is also to begin to understand the nature of the suffering we inflict on them. A herd of black and white cows with their heads down munching may not seem to be composed of separate creatures, yet in the days when the farmer's wife super-intended the dairy and the relatively small number of cows was milked by hand the individual personalities even of comparative look alikes could be distinguished and given names.

The truth is that animal personalities unfold as we encounter them on a personal level. Their responses can be stimulated by social contact or suppressed by indifference just as those of a child may be. Cats provide an interesting example of such a development. The cats of forty years ago were thought to be congenitally independent and more attached to place than people, unlike dogs. They were put out at night and so tended to sleep during the day. They were fed but except for a privileged few not much talked to or petted. Their function was to keep down rats and mice. Their social lives with humans were often little different from those who go wild.

All this has changed drastically, largely because of the widespread use of tinned cat food and cat litter which makes the keeping of cats indoors much easier so that they have now become bedsit and flat, city dwellers. In consequence, they are talked to and petted, and talk back. Their attachment in these circumstances isn't to a place but to people and they travel about in cars exchanging homes. Only people who want to distance them, and perhaps be able to abandon them, still believe that they are place rather than people oriented.

It's true that most cats if abandoned can survive at least for a time and that a cat that has moved home may get confused and return to an old place which it knows. This is largely because cats unlike dogs go out by themselves and make routes and sensory maps of their territory. The responsibility for getting home is theirs alone. Dogs are usually taken for walks and brought back again.

If we would or could allow ourselves we should find that most species where they aren't cloned by birth and environment, including the use of drugs to stimulate growth, fecundity or manageability, are expressed in recognizably unique biological units which are capable of social interaction with each other and us. The concomitant of this is of course that they also suffer uniquely and this is something which neither the factory nor the vivisector can admit.

To accept it isn't anthropomorphism but the recognition of simple biological facts, including those about our own animal nature. As a rule we use the study of non-humans to teach us things about ourselves yet if this exercise had any validity at all it must be capable of being read in reverse. If we can extrapolate from animal to man we must be able to extrapolate from man to animal. Either the vivisector must abandon the whole basis of his experimentation or he must admit that so-called anthropomorphism is a valid viewpoint though subject to the same caveats about inter-species exchangeability as must be applied to data obtained by vivisection.

We have looked constantly throughout our history for a vital qualitative difference between us and the others. Sometimes we have called what we think we have and they don't the soul, or the rational faculty or the imagination. These qualities, however interpreted, are those which are especially highly developed in humans. Yet so similar are we in our bodily construction that it's impossible to believe that they don't exist in embryo in other creatures, above all our closest kin, the other primates. Because of the language barrier, a term which we have invented for inter-cultural difficulties, we find it hard to apprehend the innate individuality of the members of other species unless we come to know them as individual companions sharing our lives and our homes.

Even language which has also been singled out as the great divider can be taught to apes by use of sign systems devised for the deaf, so that they can learn to invent, if not grammatical sentences, at least compounds. Some scientists, much like those who go on believing that cats are primarily attached to place, refuse to accept the use of human language by other primates, redefining it in the process as essentially a set of rules and relationships and downgrading the part of it which is the naming and therefore identifying of things, actions and states.

The further progress of animal rights will be slow if the ground of argument shifts each time we seem to be near to demonstrating that the difference between human and non-human is one of degree rather than kind, and especially in the matter of a common individuality. Yet recognition of the rights not of species but of the biological unit, the person, is crucial to it and must be constantly argued for. As I write, the elephant population of Zimbabwe is being culled, whole family and social groups shot to control the growing population which is threatening its own survival. This cull, carried out reluctantly and in the most humane way possible, represents the furthest we can go in animal welfare without a recognition of individual right.

CONSERVATION

Renard the runnable snouts in the dust
at the back of Deodar Road.
Behind his eyes pink coats neon
where Putney bridge halloos across the river
with hunting klaxon of Friday night gone to earth.
Chicken and chips he suppers from the daily news
ham fat, waxy skate ribs, bacon rinds.

He was out the day the gas came calling
reaching its green fingers down to his vixen and cubs
watched from a hill the men from the ministry
with their spades counting the furred lumps.
'Old dog fox I reckon he wasn't at home.'

Nothing to keep him now in the country
he headed for town, became part of the urban drift.
For a time at Richmond he lived among the mild deer
til a cracksman came fitting a bullet
between the does-eyes with a fine sense of proportion.

Myopic the old lady took him in.
She had always wanted a dog.
On Saturday he trots demure at her side
in collar and lead along the shopping high street;
evenings he spreads his red pelt
for a hearthrug. In the attic trunk
the motheaten tippet grins beadily.
The fable has come home.

When the wind rises he lifts his head.
He is waiting for the elephants already
on their way from Africa rounding the Cape like whales.
Their grey legs piston the waters
their trunks trumpet spume at the stars.
They are coming to pull down the guyropes
on the human circus and plunge the ringmaster
shrieking into the sea.

5 The Call of the Wild

When we see the human face in the dark glass throwing back the reflections of vivisector and battery farmer we sometimes comfort ourselves with that other image: hu-man the conservationist and wild life preserver. It's an essentially twentieth-century picture. Having over-run and polluted a great deal of habitat earth, like vandalizing children we are alarmed by what we have done and desperately cast around to hide the damage.

We express our concern as 'ecology', an abstraction which gives it a pseudo-scientific respectability away from the traditional interest in 'nature', landscape and its inhabitants, which can be designated sentimental, arty or anthropomorphic. It's an umbrella under which even huntsmen can hide, for at bottom it perpetuates the idea of a world which exists for man's support and pleasure.

Our efficiency as predators and pollutants has endangered our own habitat. Thousands of species of plants and animals are being made extinct every year because of toxic wastes, including the most poisonous of all – that ignorance that cuts down centuries-old rain forests to make rapidly eroding farms whose life is a few years. Now we are adding the excretions from nuclear fission which will have to be buried, drowned or shot into space because their toxic lifespan is too long for the ordinary earthly process of decay and return to the biocycle to cope with. We have made the whole earth our burrow and are fouling it irretrievably.

In doing so we automatically destroy it for every other living species of plant and animal. Until the beginning of this century our pollution could be contained in cities where we choked ourselves to death on our own fumes and excretions, but the opening up of the world with rapid transport of every kind has changed all this. So too has the expansion in man-made materials which, together with the by-products of their manufacture, aren't as biodegradable as coal, wood, wool and cotton and even iron, which can return in time to their natural elements.

Even those whose profit comes from these new developments can usually see, after years of campaigning by conservationists, the effects of uncontrolled expansion, and can be brought to make at least a cosmetic gesture in some areas of their activity. Oil companies can be made by local pressure to dress up land installations. Where there's no real focus for conservationist activity, however, it's easier for the companies to evade responsibility. They can still float oil around the world in giant drums called tankers, putting the sea and shore in constant hazard of a spillage, although even here the companies have become more careful since the great scandals of the post-war years.

In a defence of animal rights any powerful ally may have to be used and the ecology groups and parties come into this category. Many of their concerns and activities include non-human animals to some degree and especially in their intervention on behalf of endangered species. However, it should be recognized that their stance is either anthropocentric or, an approach which stems from it, in pursuit of the myth of a balanced environment.

They wish to preserve a world which humans can enjoy. The *rights* as such of non-humans have no place in this. Hunters can support the World Wildlife Fund, the National Trust and the Council for the Preservation of Rural England without feeling any ambiguity. Non-human animals are to be preserved by species for our interest, and culled when necessary to maintain an ecological balance in the area they inhabit.

This attitude reaches from the elephants of Zimbabwe I mentioned earlier, to the seals of the National Trust's Farne Islands and the gulls poisoned by the R.S.P.B. in the Scottish firths. Behind it lies the belief that it is perfectly acceptable to kill individual animals of any species in order to preserve it, either from the economic destruction of its own environment by over-crowding or from the complaints of humans with vested interests which the animal group is alleged to be damaging, usually those of fishermen or farmers.

The least successful species evolutionarily speaking, are the most attractive to the ecologist because of their very rarity which gives them that novelty humans seem to crave, and because they excite a form of crusading altruism in defence of the weak. Successful species, that is, those who aren't defeated by over-expansion but indeed may find ways of exploiting it and making a real symbiosis with us, usually end by being labelled pests or vermin and destroyed. Land gulls, urban foxes, grey squirrels come to mind at once.

We try to preserve and encourage an endangered species like the African elephant so that there will still be elephants for us to marvel at and so that they shan't be lost to our knowledge, in case we should at any time need such knowledge as part of our understanding of evolution and the universe. To the cow elephant and her calf facing the guns of an organized cull, such an explanation of our behaviour in first preserving and then killing, both at our whim, is irrelevant. We take away her life and her child's because we see them only as examples of an interesting phenomenon. Incidentally, the report of this cull contained the comment that it was thought better to kill an entire extended family herd because that leaves no elephant alive traumatized by the experience. It seems almost inconceivable that the organizers of the cull could have realized or observed that elephants are intelligent and sensitive enough to experience trauma and yet still carry on with the killing.

I will be told that such actions are necessary for the animals' own welfare. Yet it isn't an argument we would dare to use for our own species where every human life is in theory sacrosanct. We have used similar methods of genocide in the unregenerate past, of course, in order to control or exterminate pest populations of humans: the supplying of infected blankets to American Indians for example in order that the invading white man could take over their land can be seen as a human parallel to the gull poisoning in Scotland.

Once again we use death as a means of population control partly because we can and partly because the wholesale slaughter of animals for food discourages us from seeing them as individuals. If we can kill cows and calves then we can kill elephant cows and calves. It's interesting that in mitigation it was alleged that twenty-five per cent of the elephant meat went to the local human population who suffer from protein deficiency.

Kangaroos are culled in the same way in spite of their acknowledged charm and their status as a national symbol. The truth is that any non-human population which we decide to protect and preserve will, if we're successful, eventually present us with this problem precisely because we have irrevocably upset the ecological balance, which is really the working out of evolutionary principles. We know this, yet we still go on allowing populations to build up because we believe that we have the right to cure the problem by killing.

Wildness as I've indicated earlier is now a romantic and artificial concept. The elephants of Zimbabwe are no more wild than sheep or goats pastured free range on mountains, or New Forest ponies. They are managed, if not precisely farmed. This necessary management of so-called wild life populations brings with it the responsibility for their growth and for the individual lives of their members. As long as we believe we can solve all our problems in the last resort by killing, we shan't look any further for a solution.

The real answer, I believe, is embedded in the RSPCA report on feral cats. The estimate for the number of feral cats in the UK is from 12,000 to 1.2 million. The report considers five courses of action. The first is to leave a feral cat colony alone in the care of a responsible human. It applies only to rural colonies where the general public are unlikely to be involved. This option was finally rejected by the Council of the RSPCA when the report was reviewed. The second option is to eradicate the colony completely. The body of the report, however, makes it clear that this course leaves a vacant habitat which unless it is made less attractive will eventually be filled by a new colony. The same applies to the third option: to reduce the numbers by controlled culling which only postpones the problem until the colony builds up again. Pest control firms, the report notes, expect to be called on periodically where this so-called solution is adopted.

The two most attractive possibilities both use birth control; in the case of option four the spaying and neutering of cats and their return to their home site, and in option five the use of chemical contraceptives. The report *strongly* recommends option four and also recommends 'that further research into chemical birth control be carried out with a view to finding a safe and reliable drug'. The drugs available at the moment when administered in the long term carry a high risk of endometrial hyperplasia and in any case many queens find ways of avoiding them.

Killing or culling doesn't provide a long-term solution to over-population of a species because as long as there is food and space the population will always build up again, unless the actual number of births can be controlled. Yet little research has so far been done on this method because we believe we have the ultimate right to kill. The Farne Island seals provide another good illustration. It should be possible, given the knowledge of the grey seal's reproductive cycle which already exists, to intervene in what is a lengthy process at some appropriate point, for instance when the embryo is held in a blastocycst for some months, either with a contraceptive or an abortifacient drug, by implant or injection.

Once again it's a matter of rejecting the traditional solution in favour of the immediately more costly one of research which will in the long run probably turn out to be the most cost effective. The report on feral cats notes the cheapness of the chemical contraceptive method if it could be made safer and more efficient. In the case of the Farne Islands seals, that otherwise admirable body, the National Trust, which administers them has found itself committed to a policy of repeated culls every few years. The local fishing lobby has been insistent that seals are breaking their nets and eating the fish.

Culling clearly doesn't solve the problem. It makes a placatory gesture in the direction of the enraged fishermen while at the same time angering many of the National Trust's own members who are against seal hunting. It can be argued, and indeed is, that feral populations should be left alone to fend for themselves and that the laws of evolution should solve the problem by weeding out the weak, usually the young and the old, and leaving the fittest to enjoy what life the environment can support.

Most humans, however, find this distressing to contemplate and prefer the quick 'clean' kill. We operate a double standard. In non-human life it's the quality that matters; in human it's the life itself. We shrink from the thought that it would have been better for every Jew to be shot on arrest rather then endure the living death of the concentration camps yet with non-humans we believe the opposite. For humans we have to believe in hope, that things will get better, even against all rational evidence, that the deliverers will come whether in human shape or as the panacea in bottle or syringe. For non-humans we accept far too quickly that nothing can be done and the attempt to change conditions can be abandoned in death. We assume that seals must and will return to a particular place rather than consider the possibility of rehoming them.

Both seals and whales excite our compassion: they are intertwined with the human imagination, certainly that of Western Europe and then by extension North America, in folktale, song and history. Moby Dick and the Grey Silkie are quasi-human mythological figures in our culture. This isn't so for the Japanese to whom whales and dolphins are more like sea cattle than magical creatures and to whom our current preoccupation with their fate is hardly understandable. They point out, quite consistently, that the Western world eats beef in the way they eat whale and dolphin. They could also say that at least sea cattle lead a free range life.

As I write, the Green Peace organization is involved in a brush with the Soviet authorities over the feeding of whale meat to animals being farmed for their fur. Sickening as this is to a vegetarian, it's logically no more repellent than turning kangaroos or old horses into tinned pet food or giving mice to the snakes in the London Zoo. It's merely more spectacular and in violation of international agreements on whaling which have been brought about by a successful pressure group. While we must be grateful for any mitigation of the global slaughter of non-humans, as I've said before, there is still no intrinsic reason why an individual whale has more right to life than a bullock or a rat. Our defence of them is because of their grandeur and mythological place in our culture: that is, it is anthropocentric. We admire them and therefore they must live.

We like too to maintain the myth of the wilderness for our own psychological benefit, much as many Americans hark back to the frontier days as the time of true manly values when the pioneers themselves longed only for warmth and comfort and enough to eat out of the only available land. The truth is that the wilderness has gone for the foreseeable future however much, like Peter Pan, we try not to grow up and recognize it. The national park is exactly what its title implies: the large-scale descendant of the stately home's garden extension married with the municipal gardens. The sooner we recognize this and settle down to our role as park keepers rather than woodsmen the better it will be for the whole earth.

Yet the myths are very powerful and we constantly update them. A new twist has been given to the mythology of the wilderness by the threat of nuclear war. Each of us believes that we will personally survive as part of our biological urge to do so, and for many people this opens the door to survival fantasies of self-sufficiency that manifest themselves in television programmes and literature telling us how to grow and kill our own meat. The earth will become a wilderness once more and we shall be everyone their own Crusoe among the tumbled concrete of the cities. Science fiction deals with, as one of its major sub-genres, survival fantasy.

Television has itself become an extension of and a

substitute for the wild life park. The Western world has always been fascinated by other animals and in particular by the curious and the beautiful. The small screen in our homes has taken over from the beast fables and, like them, it often seems in its selection of material to be pointing to a moral. Because this is the late twentieth century the message is packaged as scientific fact bolstered by the camera which 'cannot lie'. The image presented is of nature, red in tooth and claw, where species prey upon each other for survival. The ethic drawn from this includes the concept of moral and physical carnivorousness as an inescapable fact of all animal, including human, life. It needs to be pointed out that even seemingly scientific programmes are entertainment. Their components are selected for dramatic impact, either in action or spectacle.

The picture of the universe that they show is in many ways the modern equivalent of fairyland. We observe the strange and beautiful creatures presented to us: boxed, behind glass, as we look into another world that is always on the fringe of ours. We forget that an editorial hand has been selecting and snipping among thousands of feet of film to bring us a latter-day equivalent of mediaeval romance and bestiary combined. The lives of most mammals are herbivorous and non-dramatic. The carnivores are a minority yet they are the ones who make good television. In a half hour programme the amount of time that can be given to watching a wildebeest browse or a rat forage is very short in proportion to the real animal hours expended in the primary business of food gathering. Similarly, in films about humans it's the drama we see, not the endless shopping, washing, typing, packing. Death is more dramatic than life.

The camera helps us to spy on the hitherto hidden places of the non-human world. It should give us new insights, such as, for instance, that size is relative, a necessary corrective to our usual assumptions, often unconscious, about the value of other creatures' lives when measured on the human physical scale, which leads us to admire those who are bigger than ourselves, and despise the smaller, believing that brain size and length of nerves are somehow an indicator of the ability to suffer or experience pleasure.

Instead, the editorial hand and the necessity for constant entertainment distort our understanding, often reinforcing the human sense of superiority by pointing up difference rather than similarity. The very shortness of the slots for this material encourages a behavioural approach to animals rather than the more profound study of their lives which enlightened ethologists like Jane Goodall have pursued, in particular with her work on chimpanzees and hyenas, in an effort to get beyond the merely exclamatory.

Although television should expand our knowledge of the non-human biosphere it also trivializes it, as it does so many other important concerns. Again we are using animals for our diversion and pleasure and as symbols to reinforce our own behaviour, not for themselves. Such programmes, because of their claim to a necessarily doctored authenticity, usually avoid any overt comment on what the viewer is seeing or any attempt to put it into context other than the currently fashionable one of man's destruction of the 'natural' world. The constant reinforcement of the concept of an essentially predatory, amoral universe allows hunter and conservationist to lie down together in maintaining the myth of the wild and the place of man the hunter in the evolutionary pattern.

LAG GOOSE

Tagged the bird
braked in full flight
fell out of the sky
a tumbled handsized cloud
of grey and white flake down
snow or bunched sheets in the windowed washer.
Old lag, ticket of leave
laggard in formation
the lead devil took it hindmost
out of the pinking dawn.

Now it lies on the scrubbed table
nature mort rigid with the controlled rage
of Oudry at still life.
The furled orange webs
are toy parasols that will
open and shut to a pulled ligament.
About the leg handle is a small band
  'If found return to . . .'

So you were caught before
goosey, goosey or is it gander?
Who can tell til the belly is slit?
Once ago you were lured down
by the disc jockeying cries
to the snare of our curiosity
that would follow you about your seasons
mark where you spring and fall
· where you are laid and lay.
Transfixed by the mesh and the numbing
pellet then as now you grew limp
to our will. The tag records
you twice shot, a lively statistic
plotting your graph to where you
and the winged bullet would meet
at a point called why.

Were you afraid, wary ever after
that first fix? We don't understand
the terrors of your birdbrain
our own metaphor minifies for us.
But we have always used you

quilled our poems and graced our palms
made Christmas and pantomime of you
painted you skidding down two point aheel
on some plashet of our nostalgic
first grey light among rufty-tufty reeds

Small cylinder
go tell the recording computer
our grey lag goose is dead.

6 Beasts for Pleasure

It was not Darwin's fault that they misunderstood. The shocking suggestion that each species was not individually created, that man and monkey might have a common ancestor and that all life might one day be represented as a vast family tree, when research had finally unearthed the missing petrified branches, needed some palliative. One sentence seemed to provide it: 'And as natural selection works solely by and for the good of each being, all corporeal and mental endowments will tend to progress towards perfection.' Man who had always been halfway between the angels and beasts heaved a sigh of relief. The angels had flown off leaving him with only his disreputable kinsmen but all was well, for wasn't he the top of the family tree? Ignore 'the good of each being' and concentrate on the progress towards perfection. If evolution was a forward march then man was the vanguard, the flashing spearhead. All life found its fulfilment in him. One again he was lord of all, not this time by divine pronouncement but by natural law, with dominion over all the other beasts who were only nature's byways and dead-ends as she struggled through geological time to bring forth *homo sapiens*. Over-specialized, dumb, the rest of the animals were there for his use and pleasure, superseded by his intelligence and doomed to die out like the giant reptiles. Human pride which had had its gorgeous role of king-making myth stripped from it, hurried to re-clothe itself in grey but serviceable scientific dress.

What Darwin (with his almost mediaeval vision of the infinite variety of nature) called 'the endless forms most beautiful and most wonderful' were to him subjects for study and delight. To the Royal Commission of 1875 set up to inquire into vivisection he said that he had never experimented on an animal but, with the scientist's obsession with discovery, he thought a ban on experimentation would be 'a very great evil'. It would, I think, never have occurred to him that men of science could be unnecessarily cruel, any more than he seems to have realized the thousand implications of his own work.

We have always used animals not simply for practical purposes but as metaphors for our own emotional requirements, and it's this that we are unwilling to give up by considering them as creatures with rights and lives of their own. We refuse to recognize the sentience of other species in order that we may go on treating them as objects, projections and symbols. What stands in the way of the abolition of capital sports is the lack of acknowledgement of psychological processes, our own and other animals'.

Hunting is an anachronism. Whatever practical justifications are offered for it are only a blind. All the animals hunted for pleasure, the fox, stag and hare, could be controlled by restoring or not disturbing the ecological balance, by better protection of domestic livestock and plants, by contraception and sterilization, or by deportation to other under-populated parts of the country. There is no need to cull, a euphemism suggesting the plucking of flowers. Practical problems call for practical solutions. There is need for better hen-houses and the ringing of trees that might be damaged by the onslaught of deer and for methods to keep out rabbits. Once the principle that we don't kill is law, ways will be found.

We are not in these islands neolithic predators who must kill for food and protection like other carnivores, but a highly industrialized and overconcentrated population that must try to preserve for our own sanity and relaxation an emotionally balanced economy of town and country. We need other animals as part of our background as we need unpolluted skies and rivers, trees in architecturally beautiful cities, oil-free beaches.

I realize that this is the empirical appeal to man's selfishness and as such it is rejected by many of those concerned for animal rights and welfare. But to do this seems to me not only a psychological mistake but also in a sense a piece of that pseudo-Darwinian arrogance that sees us not as other animals but once more as lords of creation. It's not simply that we should protect our weaker brethren but that we need them too, though our rights shouldn't be allowed to cancel out theirs when we think, mistakenly, that we don't.

In return for the favour of their being among us we owe them respect for their lives and feelings, however different these may be from our own. History is darkly patched with genocide bitterly repented later in times of greater understanding. We are appalled now by the destruction of the Albigensians and the American Indians; our descendents who, if given the chance, will understand animals better, may be horrified that we, seemingly so advanced with a man on the moon, rode about the country hallooing after small mammals, clubbed baby seals to death and almost killed off a whole species, the otter. The Indians seemed different, savages, beasts. We now know that they weren't. Our ignorance about other animals should make us pause.

However deep this ignorance it shouldn't for one moment allow us to assume that the animals who are being hunted don't suffer pain and fear. A sick creature is a pitiful sight in its misery and the obviousness of its suffering. The fish that got away is doubly wary, as is the bird that has been shot at or nearly taken. Any poacher knows that they learn from such an experience and it is a knowledge from the sharp school of fear. The instinct to preserve life may be greater in a less intellectual organism and the agony of losing it therefore greater too without the help of reason. The supposition that a man may die many times in imagination but a fox does not is based only on our knowledge of our own thought processes. It would be impossible to train an animal by inducing physical pain, as so many have been trained, if it didn't first feel then remember the pain, and fear a renewal of it. Only the hunters enjoy the chase.

All this may seem so obvious as to be not worth stating, although the 1951 government committee appointed to inquire into the treatment of wild animals was 'not satisfied that wild animals suffer from apprehension or the after-effects of fear to the same extent as human beings'. But whatever the degree of suffering, it is agreed that there is some. How then can men continue to hurt without the excuse or spur of hunger and self-protection? The answer is obviously in their emotional needs and hunters will admit this. We shouldn't, though, allow ourselves to be foxed by the simple view usually offered that it develops manliness, skill and patience and neither should they. All these, together with the pleasure which many feel in the outdoor life, can be got mountain climbing, bird watching, sailing or in dozens of activities in which the only life at hazard is one's own. The point of hunting is to conquer by catching or killing. Whether fishing, fowling, coursing or the chase, it has, like masturbation fantasy, two parts, the hunt and the kill even when that is symbolic as in the landing of a fish that is then thrown back.

In spite of the basic similarities in the various forms however, it's a mistake to over-simplify the meaning of hunting. The metaphor is an extremely subtle one with many variations which must be explained in detail if they and their attractions are to be understood and our need for them diverted into less cruel forms of satisfaction.

The chase, in which I am including hare coursing, is first of all clearly a ritual. The actors assemble in costume to take part in a sacrificial killing. This communal aspect makes it slightly different from shooting and fishing where the communal enters only after the kill when comparisons are swapped, sizes compared as bull sessions compare sexual prowess. The chase differs too in being patronized equally by both sexes. Shooting and fishing, although there are of course exceptions, are predominantly male sports. The costumes worn by hunters have several uses. They set the participants apart, making them a kind of priesthood or elect; they enhance the importance and excitement of the occasion and they provide the element of disguise, always a part of a ritual killing where no one person should be known to be the killer but all share the responsibility. An interesting extension of this is the use of hounds to do the actual running down and often the kill which absolves the humans even further while allowing them in a sense to pursue and murder vicariously by identifying with their substitutes, the pack.

The code cries from humans, dogs and horns all add to the idea and effect of a ritual as does the strange initiation of blooding, the keeping of a tally and the taking away of parts of the animals as a *memento mori*. Though attempts are made nowadays to soft-pedal the actual killing in reports of hunts, pictures of animals being torn to pieces appear from time to time in the national papers while at others there are accounts of hounds savaging pets and farm animals, hunts trampling crops and damaging property. It seems impossible that this should be in the serious pursuit of anything less than a man-eating tiger. What then is being pursued?

The use of dogs as substitutes for or extensions of the humans provides a clue. The hunted animal is also a substitute. And here the metaphor becomes personal and variable, for each, with certain limits, will set their own stamp on the victim, allowing the symbol to work at several levels. For some people violence and death are themselves sufficient. The desire to kill or to take part in a killing lurks in most of us. Troops taking a village in Vietnam go berserk and massacre the inhabitants; tourists queue for the bullfight; American, and at one time British, slaughter-houses welcome visitors; the curious paid the keeper to see snakes at the zoo swallow live food when feeding was withdrawn from public view; children torment insects (I did myself); public executions are enjoyed by many.

For others it is not the fact of death itself, the Ah! of release that no doubt went up after a particularly satisfying moment in a Roman wild beast show, but a more specific identification. Freud argued very convincingly that the original totem animal was a substitute for the father, a ritual killing by the sons in a body, which fits the chase very well, particularly the blooding and the keeping of mask, tail, paws for a sympathetic magic to give virility, and the constant harping on this attribute as conferred by hunting. The fox and the otter both have prized tails and no great insight is needed to divine what they represent. Even the folklore characters of these animals are phallic: the fox with its cunning, the otter in its playfulness. Their body shape too isn't hard to see as a phallus and both are traditionally sexy beasts and dwell in holes. From their own angles both men and women can find pleasure in hunting and conquering them, a pleasure that isn't accessible to reason since it's based on these strong psychological needs.

The hare by tradition is female like its cousin the rabbit. It was customarily called 'she' and 'poor puss'. As late as 1906 there was an outcry about the Eton practice of boys hunting pregnant does. Horrific as this may seem it was only the psychological extension of the image already present in the hunting of hares which is a symbolic rape. If this seems far-fetched there are dozens of examples in popular literature of hunting as sexual pursuit and the reader is referred to any unbowdlerized collection of broadsides. When a parallel has been so consciously drawn, and exploited in songs roared out in taverns by the very participants, it is a simple desire not to face facts to pretend that it wasn't so.

So important was the hare's femininity that breaking its back with the foot was (and still is) called 'dancing on the hare', the usual erotic movement of courtship being transferred to death. 'Pussy' is a long established feminine synonym. When caught the hare gave the added satisfaction of screaming with terror, unlike the more masculine fox. In common with the rabbit a crouched hare with ears laid back assumes a female shape (there is unfortunately no exact linguistic equivalent for 'phallic') added to by its softness, furriness and reputed timorousness.

> My lord was fond of sporting
> And hunting of the hare
> He has to pay ten thousand pounds
> The damage to repair;

sings a ballad collected in 1871 on an elderly nobleman who seduced a young wife, and again:

Some in the Town go betimes to the Downs
  To pursue the fearful Hare;
Some in the Dark love to hunt in a Park
  For to chase all the Deer that are there:
Some love to see the Falcon to flee
  With a joyful rise in the Air
But all my delight is a Cunny in the Night
  When she turns up her silver Hair.

Here the whole verse exploits the *double entendre* of hunting including falconry (where the lift of the bird is seen as an erecting penis), deer and hare hunting and finally, in case we are in any doubt what is being sung about, the rabbit in its unequivocal spelling 'cunny' for 'coney'. The rest of the song is a detailed elaboration of the metaphor.

That the meaning of an activity should rise into the communal consciousness only at a certain period and then sink down to allow the actors to pursue their drama without the uncomfortable knowledge of what they are doing, shouldn't deceive the rest of us. Most of us who need this particular fetish can enjoy rape either as victim or pursuer through the media of art, newspapers or pornography. We don't need to put it into practice on humans or on animal substitutes. Let it be quite clear that I am discussing a sport, an invention with rules designed to give maximum pleasure, not the provision of something for the pot to feed a starving family.

I said earlier that hunting had, like masturbation fantasies, two parts: the hunt and the kill; the build-up and the orgasm. The artificial rules of sportsmanship govern both elements but they aren't there for the benefit of the creature, since if it is caught too quickly it is often let go to be hunted again. Without the build-up there is no sport. Nor is it let go in the end except sometimes in the case of fishing. There must be real or symbolic orgasm; the fish is particularly susceptible of being used symbolically since there is always the act of taking it out of its own element and holding it in the hands. The very rituals and skills of hunting suggest the elaboration of a repeated fantasy, familiar to psychiatrists.

The same principles apply with slight modifications to the hunting of deer. Perhaps this has taken so long to die out because it can give satisfaction alternately to the desire to hunt both male and female, and because the very grace and nobility of the animal makes it even more desirable and more envied, for all sporting activity is a see-saw of these two emotions. By long tradition it is a magic beast, often endowed in folklore with the power of speech and in fact with the faculty of tears. The common occurrence of human metamorphosis into a deer in all mythologies shows how strong is the unconscious anthropomorphic identification.

Huntsmen when pressed will say that they rarely catch anything and that it's the excitement of the chase, or the thrill of a good gallop that they enjoy. The answer to this is to replace the live animal with a drag. Others, who are perhaps more honest with themselves, admit that the possibility of a death is necessary to their pleasure. Yet others are caught up in it because of their upbringing and continued participation in a certain kind of society. It is mainly still the rural rich and poor who hunt and defend the practice as part of the country way of life. A glance at a magazine like *Horse and Hound* will also show up the strong links between racing, eventing and hunting.

So deeply is it entrenched in the richest and most influential layer of our society that I believe only legislation will eventually send hunting in its more spectacular forms the way of bear baiting and cock fighting, even though it does seem to be declining in popularity among younger people. This, however, does not apply to shooting and fishing both of which are increasing their following and social catchment yearly, if not the actual numbers of animals killed.

To deprive an animal of its life or to terrorize it for our pleasure, looked at rationally, is a barbarous reversion. Why then, while the more obvious field sports decline, do these two increase? I think it's no accident that birds and fish are both creatures thought to be farthest from human beings, lowest therefore by popular definition, apart from the insects, on the family tree. Human imagination which may with a jump inhabit an intelligent mammal little removed from its domestic pets, finds the bird and the fish, more at home in other elements, beady-eyed, thin-blooded, easiest of all to consider as mechanisms, least understandable, most quickly reduced to the symbols familiar in dreams.

Both sports are relatively solitary and the confrontation is a personal one. The build-up requires patience and endurance, an acquired skill rather than one that's a matter of upbringing. For this reason they are particularly popular with townsmen and their cheapness makes them accessible to all classes. A gun or rod can stand in a cupboard whereas a horse or dog need the country, food, space and housing at great expense.

Those who are familiar with dream symbolism will know at once that the thing hunted behind these two animals is the same as that behind fox and otter. Indeed the two sports are very much alike. The duck shooter crouching among the reeds in the marshes is another form of the angler on the bank or in the stream; rod and gun are extensions of their owner, letting fly bullet and hook which 'take' the victim.

The supposition that, because they are so unlike *homo sapiens*, fish and birds scarcely feel pain is very widespread. As we are the top of the intellectual tree so we are paramount and unique in the subtlety and intensity of our emotions. Birds, it's true, make a great deal of squawking fuss at being caught which would seem to indicate fear, but fish are unable to be heard as they gasp in our thin air and their flappings and gill movements are taken as a mechanical attempt of the robot to return to its element. No one stops to ask why a fish has to be so carefully played as it struggles to escape from the usually much larger creature that has captured it. The leaping and twisting of a salmon, the tearing against the hook are not understood as the frantic efforts of a terrified being, still in its element not yet simply reacting mechanically to a rarefied atmosphere, but both experiencing and apprehending fear and pain. It is alleged too that the other animals have shorter memories. They may indeed be shorter, as on the whole so is their lifespan to which memory may be relative, but memories they have as

105

any old fisherman will bear out with his stories of the wily one that had been deceived by this or that bait before. Even if a fish is put back, which a glance through any angling newspaper will show is the exception rather than the rule, it has nevertheless suffered for the length of time it was 'played', its body may have been injured by the hook or by rough handling. It may be said that the fish deserves it for taking the bait. This is to be grossly anthropomorphic while at the same time applying the kind of reasoning that would blame a housewife who every day shopped in a supermarket for picking the tin of beans that was electrically charged at the whim of an assistant.

One of the chief attractions of fishing is undoubtedly the variety and subtlety of the metaphor. A fish can be found to suit every man's needs. Like all sports it has its ritual, indicating that it is an act of the imagination not of utility. The weighing and photographing are the tell-tales, recalling the comparisons in size and power of small boys, the whole penis folklore. The struggle is to possess magically for oneself that phallic shape. Fathers stand smiling beside curly headed boys with dangling mullet, recalling Tobias and the angel; tough young men display great congers; old men show small but crafty trout.

The increasing numbers of fishermen in particular should make us very wary. Obviously there is a strong need which is being fulfilled in this way and that is given no other immediately accessible outlet. While this is so, pleas for the suffering animals are unlikely to succeed; we are too egocentric. It is our equivalent of the circuses for those we are unwilling to educate enough to find an emotional and artistic expression (for fishing, indeed all hunting, is allied to art forms like the happening and the drama or perhaps, in its extreme solitary and meditative Waltonesque manifestation, to novel reading) which will allow them to identify and experience without needing to possess physically. It is also part of the British outdoor, back-to-nature, anti-intellectual character on which we pride ourselves against all the arguings of reason and the advance of technology. The usual paradox of all reform applies of course. Without legislation against fishing no other outlet will be sought and there will be no legislation until the long process of changing public opinion is far enough advanced. Perhaps knowing what we are really doing will help.

Meanwhile our own circuses, descendants of the wild beast show and the dancing bear, find accommodation increasingly hard and their lure declining as television provides engagements for the human performers and films of wild animals in the natural state which are more acceptable to audiences. Now almost entirely for children, it's not I think surprising that the heyday of the circus coincided with the dissemination of popular evolutionary theories.

The sports which they displayed were variations of bloody conflicts between assorted animals. What was wanted now was something more flattering to man: that his lesser cousins should be seen trying to ape him and failing and that his mastery of them should be demonstrated. Mastery came first. The wild cat tamer Van Amburgh, citing Genesis, beat his animals into submission with a crow bar, was painted by Landseer and patronized by Victoria in the 1830s. By the eighties new methods were being used of bribery and coercion, side by side with the more traditional ones, but the audience still demanded the illusion of conflict, of man by his superior intellect and will overcoming brute strength.

In training animals to walk on their hind legs like humans, dressing them in ruffs and hats and monkey suits, causing them to jump through hoops, catch balls and juggle we are making them imitate us in things which are comparatively easy for our physique or even habitual to us. This is doubly flattering. First we are the thing imitated, the master copy, then our imitators are seen to be pitifully inept and our own cleverness is underlined. It is of course not more grotesque for a man to walk on four legs than for a horse to walk on two but this would be the opposite of flattery, showing us as the clumsy beasts we are, especially since the horse would make a better putt at his impersonation than the man.

If the circus has lost its popularity with adults it is not, I suspect, because of suspicions of the cruelty necessary to

107

make an animal perform faultlessly on schedule, but because the other beasts have sunk so far below us in our estimation since the beginning of the technological age, in which they have no shaping part except as victims, that we no longer need to emphasize the difference between us and them. Now that we know that no animal but us can invent a computer we don't need the flattery of their inept humanoid imitations. So great is man's technical mastery that he no longer has to subdue a wild creature except in a personal context such as game fishing where the conflict is a matter of individual psychology.

Not so with children, and for them the circus keeps a certain appeal. Like animals they are subject to adults because of their physical nature and they have no technological mastery or control over their destinies. They are still able to identify alternately with performer or trainer, and to project their fantasies through the animals as their continued popularity in children's fiction makes clear. Children go to the circus because it is there, an anachronism in the electronic age. Without it their imaginations could be as well fed by films, books and visits to preservation parks.

For in the general overhauling of our attitude to animals the concept of beasts for pleasure must go and be replaced by something both more scientific and respectful. We have no right to such entertainment at the expense of other animals. The 'endless forms most beautiful and most wonderful' were not created for our benefit any more than our parents were, even though we are sprung from them and may be more intelligent and more advanced than our progenitors. Their lives remain their own not ours and they are entitled to a peaceful co-existence. We must resign ourselves to growing up and leaving behind the primitive magic of the hunt before we wake one morning to find that the human cuckoo has been so successful in ousting his foster siblings from the nest that there is nothing left for a future Darwin to study.

CHATTEL

Driving back from the literature festival
through Otley handsome in black stone
with white revers of painted windows and doors
I follow behind a tin truck
gaping an open vent high up at the back.
Stopped at the lights the gap is filled
with broad snout, a wet black sponge for sucking up
sweetness deep in summer grass.
You crane your head in the hole sideways to let
each eye in turn roll up at the sky.
Deep in tumbril shock you don't speak.
I know where you're going this summer's morning
and feel you know it too though how
when no one has ever come back with telltale
smell of blood and fear on staring hide?
I image though I can't see the shrunken dug
flat as a perished rubber glove.
The street is called Wharfedale View. It looks across
to where the moors throw a green quilt
for miles under a high sky. Why can't I just
draw the steel bolt on the tailgate
and let you run and run up there til you drop?
But the lights change. You turn Left; I go Right
for Leeds and perhaps I'm quite wrong
and you're just being moved on to new pasture.
Then why can't I safe home sleep
but see still your face laid along the tailgate
with one moist eye turned up questioning
whether I would have drawn that bolt
if you'd been able to ask me in a tongue
I couldn't kid myself I misunderstood?

7 Protest

The RSPCA was founded in 1824. Two years before, a vital piece of legislation, An Act to Prevent the Cruel and Improper Treatment of Cattle, promoted by Richard Martin and Lord Erskine, had provided the necessary framework to begin to counter some of the worst cruelty to animals in the England of Jane Austen and John Keats. Violence against animals was an everyday sight, as was violence against humans. Cattle and horses were brutally beaten as a matter of course and bull baiting was a popular spectacle. The Act did nothing to prevent baiting; that had to wait a further thirteen years until 1835 when the Act was widened to include conditions for slaughter as well. Yet prosecutions were begun at once against individual acts of cruelty and in the first year of its founding the RSPCA (the Royal handle was added in 1840) brought nearly 150 prosecutions, taking over the role of main agent in this field. It had taken thirty-five years since the first attempted legislation to suppress bull baiting.

The RSPCA was therefore rooted in legislation and prosecution from its beginning and might have looked forward to a vigorously combative future, both pursuing individual acts of cruelty and helping to outlaw general evils. Great things were hoped of the Royal Commission of Enquiry which reported in 1876. The resulting legislation, however, was muted and on the issue of vivisection more a protection for the vivisector than the vivisected. As if in some way this Act had exhausted the radical energy of the early reformers the RSPCA drifted in the direction of animal welfare rather than reform. Its funds came chiefly from legacies, a pattern established in the beginning when a bequest from the novelist Ann Radcliffe made it solvent in 1832 after several years of financial uncertainty. The effect of this funding source was to cause the Society to avoid public conflict and the adoption of any position which might offend benefactors and to concentrate its work on the provision of clinics, inspectors, rescue and general welfare, all necessary in themselves but, without a more radical element of activity, inclined to palliate rather than remove abuse.

Two world wars have done nothing to advance the frontiers of the animal movement; the death of millions of humans breeds a simultaneous indifference towards non-humans. In the late fifties, however, there was fresh activity resulting in the setting up of the Littlewood Committee by the Home Office to look into the administration of an Act that was now nearly a hundred years old, during which time the whole ground of animal abuse had shifted from the streets to the factory farm and the laboratory. The Littlewood Committee reported in 1965 and its findings have still not been given a full debate in Parliament let alone been implemented in an Act.

Democracy depends on the proper functioning of the parliamentary system. The governed must give their assent to an ordered society and they will on the whole in England do so, as long as the moral law doesn't seem to be flouted and as long as there is legislative progress in the particular area of concern, however slow. The failure of successive governments to act on the Littlewood report which is now nearly twenty years old has given a focus to the growing unease at our exploitation of other animals which could find no outlet in the established concept of animal welfare.

The movement for animal rights and liberation grew up, I believe, partly out of anger that Parliament on this issue seemed to be in the hands of powerful factions, mainly the medical and agricultural, which were stifling debate, but also as the natural correlative of other radical liberationist movements, particularly those for the greater acknowledgement of the rights of women and ethnic minorities. In all these movements the groundwork was laid in the late fifties and sixties by articles and speeches culminating in an aggressive new assertion, in terms of the formation of a visible pressure group or movement in the seventies.

Alternative organizations to the RSPCA had begun to emerge quite early, as soon as people began to identify separate strands within the overall fabric of animal welfare and to wish to concentrate on one of them. Vivisection was an early and obvious candidate following the deeply unsatisfactory provisions of the 1876 Act and the great rise in the number of experiments. The National Anti-Vivisection Society was founded in 1876, followed in the early twentieth century by the British Union Against Vivisection.

These two societies exemplify the danger to which radical movements are prone, that is to ideological division and in-fighting. The NAVS originally represented the extreme position of total abolition, extreme that is to the BUAV which favoured a gradualist approach. A matter of tactics became a source of internecine conflict which the animal movement has from time to time fallen into, losing both thrust and public understanding in the process.

The seeming stagnation after the Second World War was attacked repeatedly during the sixties by, in particular, Brigid Brophy whose contribution Richard Ryder acknowledges in *Victims of Science*. Finding no movement in Parliament, campaigners with various pro-animal interests began to look for alternative methods of progress. One of the first was the formation of Beauty Without Cruelty by Lord and Lady Dowding to provide cosmetics that had neither been tested on animals nor contained animal products.

Beauty Without Cruelty was an offshoot of the NAVS of which the Dowdings were active members. They correctly identified a morally ambiguous area for action. Women, and indeed men, need cosmetics. For thousands of years humans have improved on what is a basically rather dowdy format, when set against the exotic colourings of other creatures, by painting, dyeing and perfuming themselves, until today cosmetics are a multinational, multimillion pound industry. Yet many people find the testing of cosmetics on animals and their use as constituents morally offensive. Beauty Without Cruelty sets out to provide

113

acceptable alternatives that can compete commercially both in price and desirability with the international bestsellers. It also deals in fake furs on the same principle.

What its enterprise shows is that the use of animals in this area of fashion is totally unnecessary. Cosmetics can be manufactured and marketed without the death or suffering of a single animal. It also shows that animal welfare needn't by synonymous with frumpishness and misplaced puritanism, with that crankiness that used to attach as a stigma to animal lovers, and vegetarians in particular. Given the success of Beauty Without Cruelty products it's surprising that more firms haven't followed their example. In fact only Yardley among the household names produces totally acceptable substances. It has been left to smaller companies to follow Beauty Without Cruelty on a course which has been given added impetus by the health food fashion to which it's linked. The main outlet for animal free cosmetics is the health food shop.

Successful as this movement for alternatives has been it will not be able to make the next leap forward without legislation which provides for the listing of ingredients on cosmetics as well as on foods, and further pressure to make manufacturers renounce animal testing and say so on their products. In this respect Beauty Without Cruelty is an exemplar of how far we can go against a background of massive vested interest by an appeal to humanitarian principles, rather on the lines of a code of practice, without the backing of law. The NAVS through the Lord Dowding Fund for Humane Research supports another alternative approach. It selects radical research projects for financial support which don't use animals and furthers the cause of animal free research by exploring alternative methods. FRAME (Fund for the Replacement of Animals in Medical Experiments) also works along the same lines, correlating work on alternative methods, arranging conferences and publishing papers. Once again the old divisions reappear, however, between these two organizations, with the Dowding fund insisting on greater purity of method while FRAME tries to spread the anti-vivisectionist gospel among the medical profession, laying itself open in the process to accusations of woolly thinking and collaboration with the enemy. A further body working in this area is the Lawson Tait Trust established in 1961 to encourage research into alternatives.

Without the force of law, alternatives, whether to factory farming, lipstick or vivisection, must always be a matter of voluntary selection by the individual against all the pressure that the establishment can apply. Sometimes as in the case of animal based and tested cosmetics the establishment is commerce, exploiting our own fears of inadequacy and sexual and social failure; sometimes it is commerce preying upon our fears for our livelihood as farmers or our advancement in the medical profession. In every case it can be backed up by excuses such as 'everybody does it'; 'nothing can be proved'; 'I didn't know . . .' Always in the background, however, is the unacceptable face of capitalism, state or private, whose profits are made at the expense of rabbits' eyes, electroded monkeys, crated calves and pigs and those symbols of all suffering animalkind, the laboratory rat and the battery hen.

Alternatives must be found and must be ready to hand to refute that stage of the argument that rests on the 'there's no other way' theory, but alternatives by themselves can't bring about radical change on a voluntary basis because the interests on the other side are too powerful, both in terms of simple power and in persuasion by the use of advertising and by social and professional pressure. However, work on alternatives must go on unceasingly because, apart from the lives they save or make more tolerable now, they are a vital element in the final victory.

For in this field there *can* be a victory and we must and can progress towards it. Ironically, the field of animal rights is more susceptible to a complete solution than either women's rights or those of minorities, precisely because the discrimination exercised by speciesism is a physical one that requires a physical solution. In human matters it's perfectly possible to abolish legal and physical discrimination against a particular group and still be left with emotional and social inequalities which can't apply with other non-human animals.

Meat eating and vivisection, to take the two largest areas of abuse, can be abolished and substitutes found and it's perhaps partly the realization of this that has contributed another strand to the latest developments in the pursuit of a better life for non-humans: the exploration of the concept of animal rights and of how they can be achieved.

The sixties, that necessary psychological watershed which has made us able, though only just, to cope emotionally with the age of the computer and all it will mean, and with the other leaps in human knowledge which include space travel and genetic engineering, also give a new thrust among the other movements for the extension of human rights, to the concept of animal rights which had been propounded by earlier philosophers, in particular Jeremy Bentham and John Stuart Mill.

The concept that non-humans aren't just the object of our compassion and concern for their *welfare* but may be said to have rights parallel to those of oppressed human groups which struggle for their own liberation, carries with it certain implications when set in the historical context in which it has grown up after a protracted infancy. It is, I think, no coincidence that it occurred at the same time as the last great struggles against old style colonialism and particularly the war of Algerian Independence.

This political climate, coupled with parliamentary stagnation as I observed it in the late sixties, seemed to me to be a seed bed for extra-parliamentary activity which I explored in fictional form in my novel *I Want to Go to Moscow*. In particular I felt that younger people concerned with animal rights would become increasingly frustrated with the lack of legislative progress and would develop methods of exerting pressure on the establishment parallel to those used by other political groups. There was no other way for them to go.

The first extra-parliamentary recourse in a democracy where the political machinery has jammed is the letter, petition, march, demonstration in ascending order of legitimate activity. These means are built by custom and practice into that tacit constitution we accept as our system of government. They are hallowed by centuries of British practice and some of their manifestations have become part of radical history and mythology. From time to time the authorities react violently against them, making martyrs in the process and adding to the myths.

One of the effects of parliamentary inertia has been the continued proliferation of societies, parallel to the pressure groups so much a feature of seventies politics, within the animal movement to concentrate on various aspects of abuse: Compassion in World Farming, Chickens' Lib, the Vegetarian Society, the Cats Protection League, Universities Federation for Animal Welfare. Each in turn and according to its resources has employed the traditional methods of extra-parliamentary activity, organizing petitions, opinion polls and demonstrations. In this sense the animal movement has become politicized like any drive for human rights.

The latest development along recognized lines has been the founding of the Group for Putting Animals into Politics which includes the recruitment of elected MPs to the animal cause, and pressure on the political parties to make animal matters a major concern written into their election manifesto. A growing percentage of voters has expressed itself willing to switch votes in an election to a candidate supporting an improvement in the lives and deaths of non-humans.

The result of each proliferation by the end of the seventies, a badly fragmented movement which was in danger of duplication and of sapping its collective energy with moral and physical competition among the components for both public approbation and funding. Fortunately this danger was seen and two umbrella organizations were formed, Campaign for Animal Welfare and Animal Aid, to reunite and provide joint publicity for the various branches of concern and activity.

In spite, however, of all this effort and of the growing unease and desire for reforms by the public which the opinion polls, taken regularly by the organizations on every aspect of animal matters from hunting through battery farming to vivisection, reflect, human affairs and vested interests continue to keep reform from becoming law and this tendency has probably been strengthened by the renewed term of office for a right-wing government whose links are with both multinational companies and the hunting, farming landowners.

Extra-parliamentary activity as I predicted has now expanded from the exertion of pressure by legal and recognized methods into so-called 'direct action'. Ironically, too, the BUAV, which began as a gradualist organization in response to the absolutist stance taken by the NAVS, currently publicizes and supports the main group of activists, the Animal Liberation Front, while the NAVS explores the path of alternatives.

The ALF trains and operates in classic guerrilla style in a number of loosely affiliated cells whose front-line members are usually unknown to other cells and necessarily change as some are prosecuted and therefore exposed. In addition there are one or two open publicists who may have been active themselves but have had to give up illegal activity after prosecution.

Their methods are the commando-style entry of buildings where animals may be kept for vivisection or battery farming, the release or removal of as many as possible, the destruction of equipment and the painting of slogans, followed by a call to the press claiming responsibility and reporting on the condition of the animals before and after removal. Such animals as can be, mainly cats, dogs, gerbils, mice and battery chickens, are rehoused.

The ALF has a target list of blacked institutions which may be subjects of attack. They include schools where animals are kept for dissection or the study of battery farming methods, fur farms, batteries, private and public laboratories, fur shops, breeding centres and testing centres. The list itself underlines the sheer numbers and complexity of animal use all over the country, often in isolated sites away from the public eye, or disguised by the respectable face of a university or government department. Small groups now operate from the Channel to Scotland, from the English shires to Wales and the North. A study of the cuttings from local papers where their activities are usually reported shows a network of constant activity that if brought together begins to assume the proportions of a resistance movement.

Government inertia is alienating a growing number of the young and idealistic, and they are increasingly backed in their illegal action by a hitherto respectable largely middle-class group from the animal welfare movement. Funds to provide legal representation and pay fines come from this source, that is, from people who support the aims and to a large part the methods of direct action but who feel themselves not able to take an active role either because of age, physical ineptitude for commando-style raids or a lingering doubt about their rightness. To go on ignoring the issues which this combined active and passive group represents is to invite an escalation in law breaking extra-parliamentary activity.

It will be said that to 'give in' to such tactics is to invite every minority group to flout the accepted mechanisms of democracy and that that would lead to the breakdown of the parliamentary system. Against this it must be said that Parliament has itself spoken through the Littlewood Committee and been flouted by the vested interests of farmers and vivisectors and their attendant industries, and further that there is general agreement that an Act passed in 1876 desperately needs revision.

The activists have a dual purpose: to release individual animals from lives of misery and to draw attention to the need for change. There is of course a very real danger that the wilful recalcitrance which refuses to bend to pressure will be hardened by such activity but it is hard to see where else the animal rights movement can go since it has been exploring other routes to progress for a hundred years.

One person's protest is of course another's vandalism. Animals aren't their own masters but someone's property, a slave population. To 'free' them is to steal just as it was to give a runaway slave sanctuary. Breaking and entering is a statutory crime whatever the moral incentive; painting a slogan may constitute criminal damage; even demonstrating may be construed as liable to cause a breach of the peace.

Because animals themselves can't argue their own cause, activists claim the moral right to do it for them and to break the law on their behalf. In many spheres morality and the law will clash and we will be forced to make a choice. Two consenting male adults of nineteen who choose to have sex together in the privacy of their own home are committing an illegal act. On a more trivial level every motorist in the country probably breaks the law at least once on every journey.

The law isn't fixed or sacrosanct. It's subject to change and social fashion. To the liberationist, the suffering of non-humans outweighs legality and this reflects decisions which reformers have constantly had to make in search of greater justice. Trade unions were once illegal conspiracies; hunger marches for cheaper bread could be turned into riots by reading the Act. The moral imperative of women's suffrage for thousands of members of the suffragette movement justified direct and extra-parliamentary action because their voice could only be raised in Parliament itself by surrogates, and the establishment was unwilling to reform itself until forced to do so by, among other pressures, the illegal activities of otherwise respectable women.

The other militant arm of the animal rights movement is the Hunt Saboteurs Association which carries out disruption of hunts, including and perhaps especially, organized hare coursing. The Sabs, as they are called, use calls, hunting horns and aerosols of anti-mating substances to confuse both human and non-human hunters, and they use the sheer weight of physical presence to intervene in such events as the annual hare coursing, the Waterloo Cup, the Derby Day of this so-called sport. Unlike the ALF the Sabs' chief function is to be a visible presence and this has inevitably led to confrontation with hunters and police protecting hunts. Sabs are accused of violence and in such a situation are probably guilty of it. In return they are beaten up and ridden down and charged with a variety of offences including the usual behaviour liable to cause a breach of the peace.

The accusations of violence from both sides pinpoint two of the crucial problems of direct action: how far to go and how to control the chain of events. In one of their post-action telephone statements to the press a Kent group spokesman stated the ALF position: 'We have no wish to hurt people and we are not against those whose shops we attacked. But we have become frustrated with the way things are. Legal marches and demonstrations have not been recognized by the Government.'

In this case the windows of three butchers' shops and the local branch of Boots the Chemist were smashed. In another three scientists working for the Wellcome Foundation had their cars damaged with paint stripper. However, when letter bombs were sent to politicians by an alleged animal rights group the ALF disclaimed responsibility and repeated that they didn't wish to harm people or animals. Their attacks are limited to property.

It will be urged by some people in the movement that all direct action goes too far in the direction of violence. Seen from another angle the freedom fighter becomes merely a terrorist in the all too familiar mask of a balaclava. The mistake, I think, is to imagine that, on a rising scale of protest activities, there are sharp dividing lines which represent unequivocal moral choices.

Most forms of protest contain the potential for violence because they are by their nature provocative. Even the hunger striker, hallowed by Gandhian passive resistance, is a form of transposed violence where the self is put in the place of the opponent. Used in a context of violence it loses its moral purity and can therefore be resisted as merely another act of terrorism.

Each protest must be judged in its own context and assessed for potentially counter-productive results. If there is a dividing line it must, I believe, come between action against institutions and against individuals, if public support is to be increased by the protest and pressure brought to bear on the establishment. It is acceptable for paint to be sprayed on the windows of furriers but not on the fur-coated backs of humans. The Wellcome Institute is a prime target but the cars and homes of individual researchers aren't, even though it can be argued that they know what they are doing when they involve themselves in vivisection.

It has to be remembered all the time that the purpose of these tactics is to bring pressure to bear on government, not to attempt to drive thousands of researchers out of their jobs; this is an unattainable end and to attempt it or even to achieve a twenty-five per cent success would so outrage and alarm both public opinion and the governing establishment that it would be forced into an even more aggressively defensive stance, typified by the reactions to IRA hunger strikers and the Falklands invasion. Such seeming success would mean failure for the animal cause and can only be contemplated by the naïve or those whose real interest is in confrontation not in animals.

There's always a danger for any radical activist wing that some of their members' motives will be, either consciously or unconsciously, suspect. This is only to be expected, as is its mirror image: the inclusion of repressed sadists among vivisectionist researchers. For this reason, too, activities must be avoided that give too much satisfaction to any tendency to violence. I would include in this category the smashing of windows, slashing of tyres and arson. Immobilization by letting the air out of tyres, removing a vital part, or the old classic of sugar in the tank doesn't carry the same danger of psychological contamination nor do such actions raise the threshold of violence.

The question of public support must always be paramount. The public supports acts of rescue even though these still technically break several laws since they usually involve breaking and entering as well as theft. The British public knows that rescue can't take place from secure premises without such a technical illegality and it is perfectly prepared to distinguish between this and the same act committed for the purpose of burglary. It would be interesting if the evidence of a 'signing' chimpanzee could be used in court to show that the animal was confined and forced to take part in vivisection against its will. Would helping it to escape still constitute theft? I believe a British jury would probably say no.

The public, however, becomes increasingly uneasy, and rightly so, as the level of violence rises. To smash a plate glass window with a catapult can be seen as keeping the level down because of the weapon used, but such an act is always closely connected with rioting and looting. Gluing up locks and movable parts and spraying with paint rather than stripper, scuttling a boat rather than burning it seem to me to lie on the safe side of public opinion. Arson is always both psychologically and physically dangerous.

The morally unambiguous act is photography, even though it may require illegal entry. The secrecy which surrounds much of what is done to animals has no public support and to break it is one of the animal movement's most important and difficult tasks. There needs to be a constant supply of pictures from behind the locked doors. More people would come over to vegetarianism in a single night if it were possible to film undetected a day in the death of an animal from the time it enters the slaughterhouse, than by years of argument. The vested interests of the meat industry, and of drugs and weapons testing realize how powerful such a glimpse of the truth would be and make sure that as little as possible is understood by the public and that the claims of the animal lobby are unsubstantiated by pictures that would be irrefutable. *The Animals* film caused enormous anger and disquiet when it was shown on television but powerful as it was it is only a beginning. Direct action is needed to tear down the screen of secrecy.

The Hunt Saboteurs have learnt the hard way that liberationists must constantly guard against being driven by frustration into a mirror image of the violence of the opposition. Many of the hunters and their followers have been eager to 'have a go' because such a reaction is part of their whole ethos into which hunting fits. Toughness in all its disguises is, not surprisingly, a virtue among people who ride and hunt, both in humans and non-humans. It includes the use of weapons rarely handled in this country by most of the public: guns and whips.

Saboteurs have been accused of violence and aggression

themselves and both the accusation and its occasional truth are to be expected. Passive resistance tactics have to be learnt and exercised with patience and skill because the other side will not only vent their genuine anger but deliberately provoke in the hope of discrediting the protesters and with them the whole cause.

Direct action always involves the possibility of deliberate or accidental confrontation and therefore of conflict and potential violence. Motives and methods must be under constant study because at stake is a cause involving the present suffering and death of millions of creatures. Nothing must be done that will retard progress. Liberationists must keep themselves constantly under review if they are to be able to make that spearhead contribution to a campaign that is a classic spectrum of concerns and activities which must all contribute to the progress of animal rights.

There's a very real sense in which humans in Britain don't have rights either and that must make progress in animal rights always piecemeal and based on pragmatism. Because we have no constitution which lays down British human rights it's impossible simply to insert non-humans into the relevant clause or to argue from basic principles of what may or may not be done. British law is made, not given. It is constantly being changed by Parliament and precedent and by interpretation. There is nothing that cannot be said or done to a British citizen if local or central government so decrees, even though in theory the democratic process can reverse unpopular legislation at the next election. In addition, our present electoral system makes it perfectly possible for sixty per cent of the electorate to vote against the particular political stance that ultimately has an overall majority of seats in a general election and forms the government.

These features of our parliamentary and legal system make any stand on the *rights* of animals difficult and frustrating and this increases the incentive both for direct action and for the campaign for putting animals into politics. It also means that, because there is no simple one-off legislative solution; every area of animal abuse has to be tackled separately and in a variety of ways. It's important, I believe, for animal liberationists to realize this and to build that realization into their long-term strategy. The danger of the British situation is that of constant fragmentation with consequent struggle between the groups for the imprimatur of moral correctness, public support and funds.

Animal activists do right to concentrate on specific areas of abuse because any progress is better than none, but the different groups need to be involved in overall strategy and to be constantly exchanging information. Animal Aid and Co-ordinating Animal Welfare do perform these functions but there's a place for an animal conference and standing committee rather on the lines of the Trades Union Congress, to agree joint action, although the older societies might find it difficult to give up some of their autonomy to such a body and its decisions.

There's already a useful international model in the Eurogroup for Animal Welfare and its spin-off, an official Intergroup of the European Parliament. I have concentrated on the UK in these chapters and on our responses to our own problems but animal abuse neither stops nor begins at our borders. Because of the international nature of modern society and in particular the influence of the multinational drug companies we are involved in a network of global suffering that includes food animals in transit, alluringly foreign cosmetics and the medicines our NHS doctor may prescribe, which if not made abroad have often been formulated and tested there.

This international aspect expands constantly and will go on doing so for the foreseeable future. A couple of examples indicate the variety and scope of problems we can expect as countries are bound more and more into a multinational web covering the whole earth. The export of live animals for slaughter has been an identified abuse for some time, a trade which the EEC has begun to regulate but which must ultimately be completely abolished. Only the EEC can deal with this question by imposing harmonization through directives on the member states. Under the Treaty of Rome no EEC member must be at an advantage or disadvantage competitively because of a disparity between national laws. This basic principle of the Treaty can be used to prevent other members undermining a piece of national legislation by, for example, importing battery calves into a country which has banned them.

It also means, however, that national legislation, for example West Germany's attempts to unilaterally outlaw battery hens, can be frustrated by vested interests using the further appeal to the EEC. The Treaty adds another layer of legislation that must be gone through with all its hazards, but it means that if any scheme for improvement can pass this hurdle it must become law for the larger part of Europe. Eurogroup has done well to recognize this and begin to try to use it. Its danger is that the desired end can become so modified in the consultative process that no real gain is achieved, as in the case of the regulations for battery hens mentioned earlier which only improve the cage measurements for Italy.

One abuse which was brought to the attention of the first meeting in Brussels of the Intergroup typifies the growing internationalization of animal welfare: the abandonment of animals, especially dogs, on motorways during the holiday period. To deal with this there needs to be a computerized identification system linked to a temporary housing scheme that would eventually return animals to their owners and charge them the appropriate boarding fee and transport cost, though it could of course be argued that anyone who could push an animal out of a car on a motorway was unfit to have it. Life is rarely as simple as this, however. Pets do run away in fright or get thrown out by one member of the group to the distress of others. Fees could be charged, too, for rehousing where this was thought better for the animal.

This problem in its international ramifications hardly affects Britain because of our island state and our strict anti-rabies laws and vigilance, although we do experience it as an internal problem. Something which does increasingly affect us, however, is the establishment of an export trade from the UK in meat slaughtered according to Muslim rite. Both our own law and the EEC's directive on pre-slaughter stunning exclude animals if killed in accordance with religious requirements. Because of its trade with Arab countries Britain is becoming a major exporter in this particularly gruesome business.

In repeated opinion polls the British public has shown itself utterly opposed to ritual slaughter without pre-stunning. There are clearly some practices, female circumcision and infibulation is one, which a society may say are no part of its culture and indeed contrary to its notion of what is right or acceptable and which it won't allow within its borders. The argument will be, in the case of ritual slaughter, that religious beliefs will be offended and minorities discriminated against, but this I think must be faced. Certainly no such argument can be used against the banning of the export of live animals for ritual slaughter or of carcases killed in this way.

Nevertheless, councils are granting licences for the setting up of Halal abattoirs because at the moment there is no law to stop them. Only an amendment to the Slaughterhouse Act 1974 to remove the exemption from pre-stunning clause for religious groups can prevent an enormous increase in the number of animals killed in a way that flouts the clear intention of the main body of the law, not even to satisfy the requirements of indigenous orthodox Jews and Muslims but to make money for exporters.

Such an amendment would turn us from an exporter to an importer, unless the import of ritually killed meat were to be banned too, and this I suspect is the real reason behind the failure of the government to acknowledge the public wish in this area. The trade must be expanding with the connivance of the farming lobby which as I've said before cares nothing for an animal's fate once it leaves the premises.

Here again legislation needs to be extended as far as the EEC and a directive issued banning at least the export of such meat by any member state so that British animals aren't merely shipped to another EEC country for ritual slaughter, and processed on. We must learn to use not only our law and democratic process but any foreign or international legislation that can make life and death better for non-humans anywhere.

CURSERY RHYME

Flopsy bunny
your limbs fall down dead,
why did you
beat the wall with your head?

Brer Rabbit lies low
says nothing to us now
the mixytar baby
is holding his paw.

Run rabbit, run
the war is inside
the bacterial timebombs
go off when you die.

Your carcase will smoulder
and spread its ash wide
so brothers and sisters
shall bob scuts and cry

Where are our aprons
check breeches and all?
Hero Peter Cottontail
come to our call.

I am coming with Thumper
they loved him in the film
surely they'll listen
as we stagger and squeal.

They say that we nibbled
five million away
we poached off a fortune
and now we must pay.

Farewell to old England
to the coneyless coast
where the only buck rarebit
is served up on toast.

O brothers in hutches
get loose when you can
make love like rabbits
but be heartless as man.

8 Where Do We Go from Here?

At the moment our human world is based upon the suffering and destruction of millions of non-humans. To perceive this and to begin to do something to change it in personal and public ways is to undergo a change of perception akin to religious or political conversion. Nothing can ever be seen in quite the same way again because once you have admitted the terror and pain of other species you will, unless you resist conversion, be always aware of the endless permutations of suffering that support our society.

Hardly any area is uncontaminated by it in some way and to see this is to see the whole world shot through with a dark thread that must be unravelled piece by piece. The apprehension of this can change a person's whole way of life and for this reason alone many people resist it. It requires us to give up tastes, sensations, practices and customs, perhaps friends and public sympathy, in support of those who can't do us any good in return except that of their own existence.

For this reason some people will reject the pull of a full perception of animal rights or will find an awareness of it too hard to maintain with consistency. As I hope I've made clear, any steps are better than none. The scale of suffering is so vast that it won't vanish overnight. Rather it must be gradually shrunk by the private and communal abandonment of each area of abuse in turn. The battle is first with our own weakness and egotism and then with the collective manifestations of these two human characteristics, which are our corruption of basic shared animal drives for life, liberty and the pursuit of happiness: survival and reproduction.

Becoming vegetarian, the refusal to benefit by the death of another animal or to take part in the whole gigantic meat industry, is obviously the first step. If I eat meat I acquiesce in and support the whole bloody business and the animals which I may meet on a walk or see from the train windows aren't for me living, feeling creatures but food units. I must cut off my empathy from them because they may turn up on my plate, even if processed beyond recognition into frozen chicken pies or pork and beef chipolatas.

Those who become vegetarians after many years of meat eating record a difference in their way of looking at other animals. It's as if a desensitizing screen were removed from between them and us and we see them not only as more vulnerable and individual but as more palpably flesh and blood.

There was a time when to become a vegetarian meant that you were branded at once as a Shavian-style crank and expected to be teetotal and wear heavy sandals. Fortunately the American health interest in whole food and the avoidance of animal fats, has given vegetarianism a fashionable aura and it's now possible to find not only health food shops but gourmet veggie cookery books and restaurants. It's best for some people to begin slowly by phasing out different products, while others will give up overnight. Whichever suits your temperament is likely to be the more lasting. However, as I said earlier, don't despair if you slip from time to time. Any drop in the number of animals killed is worth having, not for our sake but for theirs.

Having got this far in even considering becoming a vegetarian you will probably want to be involved in some animal oriented activity. Once again you should let your own temperament have a say in what form it will take. The field is so vast and complex that some people can work best solitarily; others in a group. There's probably a group in your local area, either a branch of one of the established societies or of one of the newer protest groups like Animal Aid. If you can't find one, start one at your college, factory, church, secular society, club. If you are a solitary your best work may be in monitoring the local and national press for examples of animal abuse that need comment or question.

Television programmes in particular shouldn't be allowed

to show inhumane treatment of non-humans without letters of protest because of the widespread effect of the medium and its ability, simply by showing its existence, to reinforce the *status quo*.

A recent programme on cancer showed experiments using rats which should have provoked a flood of letters since they were both cruel and pointless. Rats had tumours implanted in them and were then subjected to stress from electrical shocks. Not surprisingly, those who were unable to avoid the constant shocks by working out that they could stop them by pressing a bar four times, turned out to have less resistance to the tumours. The programme also included research into the personalities and lives of human cancer patients designed to illuminate the part played by stress in the disease. The vivisectionist admitted that his work was a very long way from yielding any data useful to humans. The face of the rat who had failed to work out the escape mechanism was haunting in its misery.

It must always be remembered that items for inclusion in documentary programmes are chosen and edited. It's arguable that the public should see such examples of vivisection to let them understand what happens in laboratories but there's also a danger that such sights, presented without comment either during or after the programme, will breed a kind of indifference or even evoke the sensations associated with horror movies, and these reactions may be no more real or lasting than if what was being seen was indeed fiction. In particular, experiments on the much abused rat and mouse can seem merely an extension of *The Rats*, and provoke fear and disgust of the animals because of man's long association with them and their powerful psychological images.

While not wishing them to set up in censorial competition with those groups which are constantly criticizing programmes for their content of sex and violence, antivivisectionists in particular need to keep a watching brief on television's treatment of vivisection and more research needs to be done into its effect on humans and whether the screening of experiments blunts or enhances our sensibilities on this question. I suspect that sometimes the reasons for including detailed scenes of experiments have more to do with sensational journalism than with informing the public.

Those of us with an interest in politics or a party affiliation can exert pressure over our own party at both local and national levels. For a long time it was thought right to keep the animal cause out of politics but it now looks as though this may have been a tactical mistake. It has always been assumed that an involvement with specific parties is damaging to an ideal which needs to remain politically neutral, but experience in other fields, the campaign for Public Lending Right for example, has shown that it's possible to solicit party support and MPs' commitment, without losing either wing of the political spectrum. The animal movement needs to maintain a delicate balancing act in this area and to remember that politicians tend to be wholehearted in their support when in opposition but a lot less eager when they have the power to implement policy.

It would be easy if animal liberation supporters could be all either pink or blue but this isn't of course the case. High Tory can easily rub shoulders with socialist on the laboratory picket line. In a democracy such political coverage is especially important if the animal cause isn't to be entirely submerged by an electoral swing. To some extent campaigners must learn to work with whoever is in power because Bills involving animals are unlikely in most cases to be left to free votes since, if conditions are to be improved, their implementation will imply at least a notional loss of money or privilege to some powerful interest.

When the government is blue with a massive majority, progress will mainly be made by exerting pressure on the Tory backbench and discovering supporters there. The danger is that too weak legislation can delay any real improvement in conditions. MPs, and especially governments, are inclined to think that certain topics can only be given an infrequent airing, and to feel that even a bad Act ought to satisfy the lobby for change in any given area for several years to come.

Nevertheless, with all the pitfalls of putting the animals'

cause into politics and ultimately through Parliament, the attempt to use the machinery of democracy has to be made since it's only by legislative change that entrenched abuses can be ended. Activists need to consider too whether centralism or devolution would better further non-human as well as human interests. Councils have sometimes been made to act on an animal issue where the full process of central government has been too slow and cumbersome. Grass roots activity might have more impact if local authorities had greater autonomy. Councils, for example, can refuse to license slaughterhouses for ritual slaughter, and could perhaps be more easily pressurized into doing so by a local opposition. Animal matters must be an issue in local as well as national elections. There needs to be a complete nationwide network of affiliated groups monitoring local issues and exchanging information on ways of dealing with them. An expanded Animal Aid might fulfil this need.

All co-ordinating activity needs money. Indeed, the whole animal movement needs funds all the time, whether to pay fines, provide transport, set up sanctuaries or produce literature. There may be people who want to do something positive for the animal cause and whose talent is for fund raising. If so they can make an enormous contribution. Until now this aspect has been piecemeal and fragmentary with the same people being called upon again and again to support each different area in turn.

Voluntary organizations all face the danger of becoming the prisoners of their benefactors in matters of policy and it would obviously be difficult for some of the more respectable organizations to take part, but the case for the beginnings of a national budget, with a deliberate attempt to find alternative sources of funds to the small private donor, should be considered. While not wanting to see the animal movement further split, I think we should discuss the question of what I can only call blood money, levies from organizations and groupings which profit from the use of non-humans: drug companies, the tote, the food industry. The government is plainly unwilling to put money into the search for alternatives to vivisection or into improving the conditions of food animals or reducing their numbers; other ways must therefore be found to provide capital for research, for constant high quality publicity, and to provide more sanctuaries for unwanted animals, as well as for the other costs which must increase as the movement tries to keep up with the multifaceted nature of the exploitation of non-humans in the late twentieth century.

Education is obviously a vital area for activists to tackle both on a personal and a public level. Human children begin with an ambiguity of response to other animals: on the one hand they are cuddly playmates; on the other they are creatures over whom even the weakest child can exercise power. Many children are appalled when they first learn the source of the meat they have been eating. Some seem to be almost natural vegetarians. Parents are often worried by a child's distaste for flesh and force meat upon it. Vegetarians need to capitalize on this antipathy in children by letting parents know what alternatives there are and that meat isn't an irreplaceable part of a growing child's diet.

Here again money is unfortunately the key. The animal movement desperately needs a television series and Channel 4 is probably the best place for it. It could include every area of activity, and in this context a weekly vegetarian cooking spot that wasn't exclusively lentils and brown rice. Education doesn't stop with children. Such a programme could provide an antidote to the mere curiosity approach of traditional wild life programmes.

More consistent pressure also needs to be exerted on the educational establishment, including soliciting the help of the teaching unions, to remove dissection from examination requirements and therefore from schools. Some children of course enjoy it and this fact must be faced. Pre-adolescence, the latency period, often includes an interest in the, to adults, disgusting and morbid, in an emotional response that seems to couple clinical detachment with excitement, and which as a psychological phenomenon hardly seems to have been studied. It allows otherwise kindly children to mutilate insects and torments pets, and to enjoy mangled or mummified bodies as any teacher knows who has ever taken a group to the British Museum.

It's important that alternatives to accepted patterns of living should be put before children of all ages. The feminist movement has seen this and tried to influence the stereotypes of role playing for men and women which children absorb from books. Animal activists, without becoming counter-productively strident, might adopt a similar practice. There are good books written by those who have a care for animals, and sometimes specifically for the children's market, which suggest that butchers' shops aren't friendly places and vivisection is at least open to discussion. Without wanting to overload childhood with too heavy a burden of moral questioning or asking children to solve the problems of adult society I still feel that they should be presented with the possibility of a meatless, non-vivisectionist world rather than having conformity always before them, engraining habits they may later find hard to break. In this, as in other areas, schools should be prepared to consider the pro-animal case and should be willing to accept leaflets designed for their particular age range, films and visiting lecturers.

It will be said that children mustn't be indoctrinated, yet they are subjected to a constant bombardment from the other side, not only in the form of received practice in our society but as a stream of advertising, particularly from the factory farming industry which makes every attempt to disguise the true origins of its products with slogans that imply an old fashioned country open air goodness and freshness, rather than the airless, artificially lit shed or cage which is the reality.

One of the most cheering phenomena of the past decade has been the growth of animal rights groups in colleges or universities. It sometimes seems as if, disenchanted with traditional radical politics, many young intellectuals have channelled their natural idealism into the pro-animal cause. It's often from these groups that the most active protesters come, quite simply because they still have the physical strength and energy and are often free of domestic and work obligations. This isn't in any sense to denigrate their contributions; they could after all be demonstrating on the other side or for any of the many other ideals, political, ethical or social which are still unrealized, but it does pose a propaganda and therefore a tactical problem. Just because of their coincidental prominence, it's possible for the opposition to use the label 'trendy lefties' or 'layabouts' or whatever is the current pejorative, in an attempt to discredit the arguments on behalf of non-humans. Organizers of demonstrations and protests should have this consciously in mind and organize their protests with as wide a range in age, class and sex as can be mustered. As it is, pro-animal demonstrations are often peopled by middle-aged women, children and young men whom the public can easily be made to identify as students. This is especially true of small protests on cold wet days. It reflects living conditions for humans in our society rather than the strength of feeling about the lives of non-humans among all sections of the population.

There's a sense, of course, in which the age, class or sex of the personnel shouldn't and doesn't matter but since our activity isn't for ourselves but for thousands of mute fellow creatures and we have their future constantly in our hands, it's our responsibility to present their case as forcefully as possible, bearing in mind that our actions can be constantly misrepresented. It is the animals and their fates that matter, and yet we are only human and our motives for taking up the animal cause will be mixed with all kinds of self-gratification which may warp our judgement and which we must guard against.

Many genuine sympathizers will feel unhappy at and psychologically unable to take part in public protests. Unless masochism is your real bent there's no point in resentfully forcing yourself into modes of action that are alien to you. The danger of eventual revulsion and the rejection of a pro-animal stance is too great. It's important not to over-strain your own emotional resources because of humankind's collective guilt. Better to stay a low profile private vegetarian than to risk relapsing into carnivorous carelessness because of your own overkill.

One of the great achievements of the last decade and a half has been to make animal rights an almost respectable issue in the sense that not only has the threshold of public consciousness been raised about animal suffering but the whole debate has been taken out of the drawer where the more extravagant causes are kept in the public mind: flat earthism, astral bodies and similar exotic concerns.

This momentum mustn't be lost. The main dangers are, as always to any radical cause, public inertia, the power of vested interests and in this case the inability of the animal rights movement to keep up with the pressure and to make the next step forward which I would liken to a private company going public. Since movement is unlikely to come from the government, it must come from the pro-animal groups themselves, if more and increasingly desperate manifestations of direct action aren't to lose what's been gained by ultimately alienating public opinion as the activities escalate in an assault on governmental indifference and collusion.

What we want and must struggle for is nothing less than the world turned upside down to the point where no animal is killed except as an act of humane euthanasia. We have to move towards this by gradual steps. The next step we need to take is deeper into politics, into the means of getting information to the public and changing its collective attitude, yet without abandoning the day-to-day welfare services that help so many thousands to survive. To do this I think we need greater co-ordination within the movement, enhanced status and funding, yet without any loss of that grass roots concern that sends people out in the morning with plastic bags of scraps to the nearest feral cat community or into the laboratory at night to free a smoking beagle.

There's no simple instant solution and most of us may not see the abolition of vivisection or an end to the massive slaughter of food animals in our lifetime. The great danger is that we humans will become discouraged and abandon our fellow creatures to that dark side of our nature that exploits and abuses them. We must expect to be pushed back from time to time and to have to pick up the pieces of the animal cause and re-form, and again this is a reason to try to make a big leap now to the point where it's hard, if not impossible, for the pro-animal campaign to be ignored or discredited. I have tried to indicate the lines along which I think this might be done. I don't expect that everyone in the pro-animal camp will agree with all or perhaps much of what I have said, but at least let it be another peg to inch the debate forwards.

Appendix A

The following are entries from the Animal Liberation Front file showing the scope and extent of direct action taken in the first six months of 1983.

15 January 1983, London
Windows of several West End furriers broken with catapults.

15 January 1983, Birmingham area
Sixty hens rescued from battery egg farm by ALF activists. They are now all in good, free range homes.

16 January 1983, Guildford, Surrey
Anti-vivisection raiders cut their way into the grounds of the Ministry of Agriculture's Infestation Control Laboratory at Tangley Place, Worplesdon Road in the early hours of the morning and rescued two foxes from their cages. The laboratory is registered to carry out painful experiments on animals.

The raiders, who later claimed the foxes had been taken to a sanctuary in the West Country, also painted anti-vivisection slogans on laboratory buildings.

21 January 1983, Badsworth, Yorkshire
ALF activists caused damage to several vehicles at the Badsworth Foxhunt Kennels in Yorkshire. Two activists were later arrested and one has since appeared in court and has been ordered to pay several hundred pounds by the magistrates.

2 February 1983, Marston, Cheshire
Thirty rabbits due to be slaughtered for the fur trade

were rescued by ALF activists from Hy-Lyne Rabbits Ltd, Marston, Cheshire. They were all taken to good homes.

10 February 1983, Macclesfield, Cheshire

Windows and walls of shop selling bloodsports equipment daubed with slogans by ALF. Locks glued up. Damage came to £300. Shop has now had new windows and door fitted at great expense.

12 February 1983, ALF action in Nottingham

Locks glued at two offices of Boots' animal research labs in Pennyfoot Street, and two windows smashed using catapults.

Catapult used to smash main plate glass window and window in door at main Boots the Chemist's shop in the town centre.

Locks of Lafayette fur shop glued and window in a fur shop in the Hockley district smashed by catapult.

13 February 1983, Chelmsford, Essex

ALF activists painted anti-fur trade slogans on a fur shop in Chelmsford, Essex. Window of shop was smashed.

14 February 1983, Seven arrests at demo

Seven people were arrested during a demonstration by animal welfare protesters at an Essex research laboratory yesterday.

Three hundred people marched from Chelmsford town centre to the Life Science Research laboratory at Stock where the arrests took place.

Technology 2 Defence Fund

In the early morning of Monday 14 February, two Glasgow activists were arrested near the animal house of the College of Technology in Glasgow.

This establishment has carried out behavioural experiments on lemurs. Rodents have also been used in toxicity tests.

15 February 1983, Piccadilly, London
ALF activists smashed windows of Rene fur shop in Dover Street, near Piccadilly, London.

17 February 1983, Morden, Surrey
ALF activists broke window of Richardsons butcher's shop.

18 February 1983, North Ockenden, Essex
ALF raiders rescued thirty hens from battery cages at Lower Meadow Farm, North Ockenden, Essex.

The raiders caused severe damage to a lorry used in the farm's battery egg business.

26 February 1983, Chelmsford, Essex
ALF raid on Quilters Farm near Chelmsford, Essex, where thousands of chickens are being raised in cramped intensive conditions.

Damage caused to water pipes and generators in empty broiler house to prevent it being restocked with more chickens.

End of February 1983, Melton Mowbray, Leicestershire
ALF activists broke windows of slaughterhouse in Melton Mowbray, Leicestershire as a protest against cruel methods used to kill animals.

3 March 1983, Dog rescued
ALF activists rescue a dog which was tied up in a shed in appalling conditions, and with a serious wound on its back. Now in a good home. RSPCA refused to prosecute despite ample evidence.

4 March 1983, Dogs rescued
Two lurcher dogs rescued by ALF from premises of man who was going to send them to a vivisection lab. The dogs were in poor condition and covered in sores. They are now in good homes.

6 March 1983, Finsbury Park, N. London
ALF activists stuck up locks of butcher's shop and meat centre with superglue.

15 March 1983, Piccadilly, London
ALF activists glue up locks and damage window of Jeunesse Et Or fur shop in Mason's Yard.

4 April 1983, Morden, Surrey
ALF activists paint slogans 'Want Cancer – Eat Meat' and 'Meat is murder' on walls of Richardsons butcher's shop.

4 April 1983, Swineshead, Lincolnshire
ALF activists destroyed a large number of snares that had been set to kill small wild animals.

8 April 1983, Sandiacre, Derbyshire
ALF activists broke two windows, painted anti-vivisection slogans on walls and windows and glued up locks at Strand Scientific Ltd in Bridge Street.

This company manufactures equipment for use in animal experiments. They had to employ workers throughout Saturday and Sunday to repair the damage and have now had to take on extra security staff.

10 April 1983, Nottingham
ALF activists painted anti-vivisection slogans at Boots the Chemist's shop at Broad Marsh, Nottingham, in protest against the experiments on animals carried out at Boots' laboratories.

10 April 1983, East Midlands area
Shed used by pet thief to store stolen animals for supply to vivisection labs and the fur trade damaged by ALF activists.

Car used by another pet thief to steal animals painted with anti-vivisection slogans by the ALF.

14 April 1983, Oldham, Lancashire
ALF activists carried out raid on H. G. Rabbitry near Oldham, Lancashire and rescued eighteen New Zealand white rabbits which were due to be sent to vivisection labs. All the rabbits are now in good homes.

21 April 1983, Brighton, Sussex
ALF activists rescued two rabbits from the Sussex University Agricultural Research Centre, where painful experiments were carried out on animals.

21 April 1983, Derby
Machine valued at about £5,000, used for killing animals for dissection, removed from Lonsdale College and destroyed by the ALF.

22 April 1983, Nottingham
Windows of two fur shops broken by ALF. Anti-fur trade slogans also daubed on shops and locks glued up. Butcher's shop also daubed and glued.

22 April 1983, Islington, N. London
Two windows of taxidermist's shop (which stuffs wild animals killed by hunters) broken with catapult.

23 April 1983, Sandiacre, Derbyshire
Another attack on Strand Scientific Ltd (manufacturers of equipment for vivisection). Anti-vivisection slogans daubed on buildings.

23 April 1983, Derby
ALF activists broke windows of Sovereign Furs with catapults.

ALF activists also carried out a swift raid on the fur department of Debenhams, splashing red ink (symbolic of the blood of animals slaughtered for the fur trade) on carpets and other fittings.

143

24 April 1983, Dagenham, Essex
ALF activists painted several six feet high slogans (such as:
'May and Baker Tortures Animals', 'Animal Belsen', and
'Imprisoned Without Trial') on the outside wall of May and
Baker animal research laboratories at Dagenham, Essex.

27 April 1983, ALF actions in Nottingham
Leather Land (fur shop): locks glued
    Firm that makes machines for stitching up fur coats: locks
      glued, slogans painted.
    The Saddlery (leather shop): locks glued, slogans painted.
    Cleaver Meats (butcher's shop): locks glued.
    Arctic Furs (fur shop): locks glued, slogans painted.
    Parr & Co. (butcher's shop): locks glued, slogans painted.
    Smith Englefield (leather shop): locks glued, slogans
      painted.
    Skincraft (fur shop): locks glued.
    Lafayette (fur shop): locks glued, window smashed.
    Vicky's (fur shop): locks glued, slogans painted.
    Also, stink bombs were thrown into Boots the Chemist's
shop in Broadmarsh as a protest against the experiments on
animals carried out at Boots' laboratories.

2 May 1983, Hanningfield Reservoir, Essex
Fifteen snares set around a wood to destroy foxes and other
wild animals destroyed by ALF activists.

3 May 1983, Nottingham ALF actions
Doors of Boots' laboratories, Pennyfoot Street (where
experiments are carried out on animals) smashed.
    Lafayette fur shop in Clumber Street, Ralphs fur shop in
Carrington Street and Skincraft fur shop in Market Street
all had windows smashed using a catapult.

9 May 1983, Newmarket
ALF activists threw red paint over outside of Deborah's fur
shop as a protest against cruelty involved in the fur trade.

11 May 1983, Cambridge
ALF activists threw red paint over windows of Joshua Taylor's shop (which has a large fur department) and glued up the door locks.

14 May 1983, Prestbury, Cheshire
Two hens, in very bad condition, rescued from cages at Devon Eggs Battery Farm during a demo by the Macclesfield branch of the Northern Animal Liberation League.

Four people were arrested and charges vary from Breach of the Peace to Obstruction and Theft.

15 May 1983, Worcester
ALF activists broke window of Crimpers International fur shop with catapult.

19 May 1983, Derby
Two butchers' shops daubed with slogans, and locks glued, by ALF activists.

19 May 1983, Cambridge
ALF activists daubed two butchers' shops with red paint and slogans such as 'Meat Means Murder'.

22 May 1983, Derby
ALF activists damaged locks of two butchers' shops so badly that padlocks had to be fitted. Later, ALF group replaced these with other padlocks, so that delay in opening the shops was caused.

23 May 1983, Derby
Outside of Lafayette fur shop paint-daubed and sign above shop damaged by ALF.

25 May 1983, Derby
Lafayette fur shop once again paint bombed by ALF activists, and daubed with anti-fur trade slogans. Leather World leather shop also paint bombed.

28 May 1983, Boston, Lincolnshire

ALF activists glued up locks of butchers' shops and caused damage at the Frans Buitlaars slaughterhouse. The slogans 'Meat Means Murder' and 'ALF' were daubed on the slaughterhouse.

Phoenix Egg Farm, where hens are imprisoned in battery cages, was also attacked. The slogans 'Belsen' and 'Chickens Lib' were daubed on buildings and the windscreen on the van was also painted out.

28 May 1983, Stone, Staffordshire

ALF activists broke windows of slaughterhouse and painted anti-meat trade slogans.

28 May 1983, Nottingham

ALF activists broke window of Halal butcher's shop and daubed slogans in protest against ritual slaughter.

31 May 1983, Sturminster Newton, Dorset

ALF activists rescued thirty-seven chickesn from factory farm conditions at Tophill Farm, Sturminster Newton, Dorset.

ALF comment: raiders who entered a North Dorset broiler house during the night stole thirty-seven almost fully grown cockerels. When they left Mr Raymond Upshall's Tophill Farm, Sturminster Newton, the letters ALF were daubed in paint on the outside doors.

10 June 1983, Derby

A supermarket freezer department had mock blood deposited around its meat section in protest against factory farmed meat (including veal) being sold in the store.

11 June 1983, Nottingham

ALF activists smashed windows of Tony's butcher's shop in Denham Street in protest against ritually slaughtered meat sold on the premises.

12 June 1983, Morden, Surrey
ALF activists glued up locks of butcher's shop and painted anti-meat trade slogans.

15 June 1983, Bilsthorpe, Nottinghamshire
ALF activists caused damage to empty battery unit sheds at Inkersol Grange Farm. The sheds were due to be used for the confinement of hens in small cages for the production of eggs for the Daylay Company.

20 June 1983: Burntcommon, Surrey
ALF activists carried out a raid on Tythbarns Farm, Burntcommon, near Woking, Surrey.

Thirteen young chicks, due to be reared for slaughter in intensive broiler conditions, rescued.

Damage carried out to Range Rover used by farmer in his factory farm business.

Jailed Animal Rights Campaigners Granted Bail
Four animal rights campaigners who were jailed on 3 June for their part in an Animal Liberation Front raid have now been released on bail pending appeal after spending about ten days behind bars.

Steve Davis (sentenced to six months' imprisonment), Mark Corsini (four months' detention), Linda Harman (twenty-one days' imprisonment), and Chris Davis (twenty-one days' imprisonment), were convicted at Chelmsford Crown Court on criminal damage and conspiracy to steal charges in connection with the ALF raid (codenamed 'Operation Valentine') on Life Science Research Laboratories at Stock, Essex, on 14 February 1983, when £76,000 worth of damage was caused and beagles, rats and mice were rescued from painful experiments.

Steve Boulding (sentenced to fifteen months), and Peter Sales (six months), also sent to prison in connection with the raid are still inside, but it is hoped that an application for bail for them will be made soon.

Nine more people are due to be sentenced on 24 June.

Appendix B: Principal Animal Rights and Welfare Organizations

Animal Rights

Animal Activists, P O Box 8, Chorlton, Manchester M21 2JP

Animal Protectors Defence Group, 91 Home Close, Hockwell Ring, Luton, Beds LU4 9NS

Animal Rights Association, 18 Annandale Road, London SE10 0DA

Animal Rights, 5 Hilsdon Drive, Shildon, County Durham DL4 2DF

Animal Vigilantes, 24 Salisbury Street, Fordingbridge, Hants SP6 1AF

British League for Animal Rights, 5 Aysgarth Road, Dulwich Village, London SE21 7JR

Gravesend Animal Rights Group, Top Flat, 21 Harmer Street, Gravesend, Kent

Animal Liberation

Animal Liberation Front, Box 190, 8 Elm Avenue, Nottingham

Eastern Animal Liberation League, c/o Oak Villa, Newton St Faiths, Norwich

Northern Animal Liberation League, Gate House, 41 Church Gate, Bolton, Lancs BL1 1HF

Southern Animal Liberation League, as above.

Animal Welfare

Action for Animals, 12 Newham House, Manor Fields, London SW15

Animal Protection Association, 21 Warwick Court, Burley Lane, Horsforth, Leeds LS18 4TB

Cats Protection League, 20 North Street, Horsham, West Sussex RH12 1BN

Compassion For Animals, 1 Commercial Road, Tunbridge Wells, Kent

Co-ordinating Animal Welfare (CAW), P O Box 61, Camberley, Surrey GU15 4EN

East London Protection for Animals, 414a Roman Road, Bow, London E3

International League for the Protection of Horses, P O Box 166, 67a Camden High St, London NW1 7JL

Lancashire Animal Welfare, 48 Kilworth Height, Fulwood, Preston, Lancashire PR2 3NX

RSPCA, The Causeway, Horsham, Sussex

St Andrew Animal Fund, 10 Queensferry St, Edinburgh EH2 4PG

Universities Federation for Animal Welfare, 8 Hamilton Close, South Mimms

Wild Animal Preservation Society, The Lee Centre, 1 Aislibie Road, Lee Green, London SE12

Bloodsports

Council for the Prevention of Cruelty by Angling, P O Box 14, Romsey SO5 9NN

Humane Action, P O Box 205, Sheffield S1 1BW

Hunt Saboteurs Association (HSA), P O Box 19, London SE22

East Midlands Hunt Saboteurs, 4 The Maltings, Shardlow, Derby DET 2HH

S E Essex Hunt Saboteurs, P O Box 47, Leigh-on-Sea, Essex

International Council Against Bullfighting, 13 Graystone Road, Tankerton, Kent CT5 2JY

League Against Cruel Sports, 83–87 Union St, London SE1 1SG

National Society for the Abolition of Cruel Sports, 33 Forest Rise, Jarvis Brook, Crowborough, East Sussex TN6 2EP

Rock Against Bloodsports, P O Box 73, Southampton, Hants SO9 7EU

Society for the Abolition of Bloodsports, 1 Newton St, Piccadilly, Manchester 1

Save Our Stags, 1 Guernsey Avenue, Broomhill, Bristol BS4 4SH

Circuses

Captive Animals Protection Society, 17 Raphael Rd, Hove, Sussex BN3 5QP

Circus Hassani (Europe's only non-animal circus), Press Officer: Mrs Thelma How, 2 North Holmes Close, Roffey, Horsham, West Sussex

Factory Farming

Chickens' Lib, 6 Pilling Lane, Skelmanthorpe, Huddersfield

Compassion in World Farming, 20 Lavant St, Petersfield, Hants

Farm and Food Society, 4 Willifield Way, London NW11 7XT

Free Range Egg Assoc., 39 Maresfield Gardens, London NW3

Protect Our Livestock, 10 Pilford Avenue, Cheltenham, Glos

National Society Against Factory Farming, 42 Mount Pleasant Rd, London SE13

Species Protection, General

British Butterfly Conservation Society, Tudor House, Quorn, Leics LE12 8AJ

Fauna and Flora Preservation Society, c/o Zoological Society of London, Regents Park, London NW1 4RY

International Fund for Animal Welfare, Tubwell House, New Road, Crowborough, E. Sussex TN6 2QH

International Primate Protection League (UK), 19–25 Argyll St, London W1V 2DU

People's Trust for Endangered Species, 19 Quarry St, Guildford, Surrey GU1 3EH

Royal Society for the Protection of Birds (RSPB), The Lodge, Sandy, Bedfordshire SG19 2DL

Wildlife Trade Monitoring Unit, IUCN Conservation Monitoring Centre, 219c Huntingdon Rd, Cambridge CB3 0DL

World Forest Action, 6 Glebe St, Oxford

World Wildlife Fund, Panda House, 29 Greville St, London EC1N 8AX

World Society for the Protection of Animals (WSPA) 106 Jermyn St, London SW1 6EE

Badgers and Otters

Cornwall Badgers Protection, 3 Lower Sharptor Cottages, Henwood, Liskeard

Croydon Badger Protection Group, 63 Harewood Gardens, Sanderstead, Surrey

Dartmoor Badgers Protection League, Spitchwick Manor, Poundgate, Devon TQ13 7PY

Gwent Badger Group, 28 Clays Road, Sling, Coleford, Glos GL16 8LJ

Joint Otter Group c/o SPNC, The Green, Nettleham, Lincoln LN2 2NT

Northumberland Badger Group, Plessey Woods Country Park, Nr Bedlington, Northumberland

Wirral Badger Protection Group, 105 Fishers Lane, Pensby, Wirral

Seals and Whales

Animal Protection Association, 1 Claremont, Newlaithes Rd, Horsforth, Leeds LS18 4LG

Dolphin Defence, Meade House, Limerstone Rd, Brighstone, Isle of Wight

International Dolphin Watch, 'Dolphin', Parklands, North Ferriby, Humberside HU14 3ET

Leicester Whale Group, 44 Hidcote Rd, Oadby, Leicester

Leviathan, 6 Elizabeth Close, Ivybridge, Devon PL21 0LG

Marine Action Centre, The Bath House, Gwydir St, Cambridge, CB1 2LW

Portsmouth Save the Whales Action Group, 97 Toronto Rd, Portsmouth, Hants

Save Our Seals, c/o 7 Thyme Court, Lumbertus Estate, Northampton NN3 4HY

Sea Shepherd Fund, 3 Rosehill, Torrance, Glasgow G64 4EW

Seals Preservation Action Group, The Green, Scarton, Longhope, By Stromness, Orkney KW16 3PQ

Southern Whale Group, 4a South Rd, Springbourne, Bournemouth, Dorset

Whale People, 171 Peckham Rye East, London SE15

Vegetarianism

Bristol University Vegetarian Society, c/o David Robinson, 18 Hampton Park, Redland, Bristol BS6 6LH

Gay Vegetarians, 49 Pratt St, London NW1

Jewish Vegetarian Society, 855 Finchley Road, London NW11 8LX

Vegetarian and Animal Liberation Society, 12 Antigua St, Edinburgh EH1 3NH

Vegetarian Society, 53 Marloes Rd, London W8 6LA

Vegan Society, 47 Highlands Rd, Leatherhead, Surrey

Wholefood School of Nutrition, 12 Coton Lane, Erdington, Birmingham 23

Vivisection

Animal Aid, 7 Castle St, Tonbridge, Kent

British Union for the Abolition of Vivisection (BUAV), 16a Crane Grove, Islington, London N7

The Lawson Tait Trust, 29a Bramhall Lane, South Bramhall, Stockport, Lancs

National Anti-Vivisection Society (NAVS), 51 Harley St, London W1N 1DD

Scottish Anti-Vivisection Society, 121 West Regent St, Glasgow G2 2SD

Scottish Society for the Prevention of Vivisection, 10 Queensferry St, Edinburgh, EH12 4PG

Alternatives

Beauty Without Cruelty, 11 Limehill Rd, Tunbridge Wells, Kent

Fund for the Replacement of Animals in Medical Experiments (FRAME), 5b The Poultry, Bank Place, St Peter's Gate, Nottingham

Humane Research Trust, Brook House, 29 Bramhall Lane South, Bramhall, Stockport, Cheshire SK7 2DN

Lord Dowding Fund for Humane Research, 51 Harley St, London W1N 1DD

Environment

Ecology Party, 36/8 Clapham Rd, London SW9 0JQ

Friends of the Earth, 377 City Rd, London EC1

Greenpeace Ltd, 36–36a Graham St, London N1 2XJ

Greenpeace (London) 6 Endsleigh St, London WC1

International Institute for Environment and Development, 10 Percy St, London W1P 0DR

Political Ecology Research Group (PERG), 34 Cowley Rd, Oxford

Women's Ecology Group, 9 Chestnut Way, Godalming, Surrey GU7 1TN

Further Reading

General Books on Animal Rights

Animals and Why They Matter Mary Midgeley, Penguin Books, 1983

Animals Are Equal Rebecca Hall, Wildwood House, 1980

Animal Liberation Peter Singer, Thorsons, 1983

Animals, Men and Morals S. and R. Godlovitch and J. Harris (eds), Gollancz, 1972

Animal Rights Considered in Relation to Social Progress Henry S. Salt, Centaur Press, 1983

Animal Rights Andrew Linzey, SCM Press, 1976

Animal Rights: a Symposium D. Paterson and R. D. Ryder (eds), Centaur Press, 1979

Extended Circle, The, Jon Wynne-Tyson (ed), Centaur Press, 1983

Fettered Kingdoms John Bryant, 1982

Man and the Natural World Keith Thomas, Allen Lane, 1983

Farming, Food and Vegetarianism

Animal Factories Jim Mason and Peter Singer, Crown (New York), 1980

Animal Machines Ruth Harrison, Stuart, 1964

Food for a Future Jon Wynne-Tyson, Centaur Press, 1975

Vivisection and Medicine

Alternatives to Pain Dallas Pratt, Argos Archives USA, 1980

Cured to Death Arabella Melville and Colin Johnson, Secker and Warburg, 1982

Dark Face of Science, The, John Vyvyan, Michael Joseph, 1971

Diseases of Civilization, The Brian Inglis, Paladin Books, 1983

Doctors on Trial John S. Bradshaw, Wildwood House, 1978

Health Shock Martin Weitz, David and Charles. ND

In Pity and In Anger John Vyvyan, Michael Joseph, 1969

Limits to Medicine Ivan Illich, Penguin, 1977

Role of Medicine, The Thomas McKeown, Basil Blackwell, 1979

Scientific Conscience, The Catherine Roberts, Centaur Press, 1974

Slaughter of the Innocent Hans Ruesch, Futura, 1979

Victims of Science Richard D. Ryder, Centaur Press, 1983

Bloodsports

Hunt and the Anti Hunt, The Philip Windeatt, Pluto Press, 1982

Outfoxed Mike Huskisson (available from the League Against Cruel Sports), 1983

Index

INDEX